MONARCH NOTES

SO-AEU-659

Sir Thomas More's
UTOPIA

JOHN W. ELLIOTT
DEPARTMENT OF ENGLISH
FAIRLEIGH DICKINSON UNIVERSITY

MONARCH PRESS

CONTENTS

THE LIFE OF THOMAS MORE AND THE
HISTORICAL BACKGROUND OF *UTOPIA*

The support of Erasmus, the famous humanist scholar of More's time, is not necessary for the confession that Thomas More is too deep, too rich a human reality for a simple biography—indeed, as Erasmus clarified, he is too deep, too rich for a *complex* biography. Many students of Thomas More's life and works, many zealous admirers of this great man, have sought to preserve his mind and spirit; and so, we have a library of books about Thomas More.

What follows is the barest outline of More's life. Any biographical study that approaches the comprehensive must confront More within the historical context of his time, and his era was one of tumultuous change and development. Even more than Francis Bacon, the harbinger of the new scientific method, the author of *Utopia* is a transitional figure; in many ways he is at the end of what we know as the Middle Ages and at the beginning of what we have learned to call the Renaissance, even though any alert student of history will know that the Middle Ages were not all dark and that the Renaissance was not all light.

MORE'S FAMILY RELATIONS AND EARLY LIFE: Thomas More could not make a claim to renowned ancestry, but his family was of good and respectable heritage and accomplishment. Thomas More's father, John, carried after his name that treasured title of the times, *gentleman*. J. H. Lupton has included the Latin phrase *non celebris, sed honesta* for More's family; More's own legend for his tomb says the same thing. His family was not famous, but it was from honest stock.

R. W. Chambers, in a chapter of his book on More, a chap-

ter sub-titled "Father and Son," has made some interesting
clarifications about More's birth. He corrects the usual birthday
of Thomas More from 7 February 1478 to 6 February 1478.
Thomas More's father had preserved in Latin, still in that time
the "official" language (but soon to be replaced by English),
the event of his son's birth:

> Memorandum, that on the Friday next after the Feast of
> the Purification of the Blessed Virgin Mary, between two
> and three in the morning, was born Thomas More, son of
> John More, gentleman, in the seventeenth year of King
> Edward, the Fourth after the Conquest of England.

Mr. Chambers shows the problem in the proud father's memo-
randum to be an insertion that reads, "to wit, the seventh day of
February." It is not a colossal difference, but the error made
by John More, gentleman, when researched, as Mr. Chambers
reminds us, reveals that More's year of birth was the year of
the first book printed in England. This was the seventeenth
year in the reign of King Edward IV.

Thomas More had three sisters and two brothers: Joan More,
born 11 March 1475; Agatha More, born 31 January 1479;
John More, born 6 June 1480; Elizabeth More, born 22 September 1482.

John More brought up his family in London, perhaps in Milk
Street, Cripplegate, perhaps in St. Giles, Cripplegate.

MORE'S FORMAL SCHOOLING: The leading school in London in More's time was St. Antony's. Nicholas Holt was school-
master at St. Antony's, and it was there that More was educated
in the disciplined Latin ways of the times. It was at St. Antony's
that Thomas More first learned of the technique of intellectual
argument that we know as debate. The technique was to find
vivid application in More's writings: we need only sample
Utopia for illustration of the fact. A sixteenth-century writer by
the name of John Stow left the following record of the educational procedures at St. Antony's School, a school noted for its
capable scholars:

The arguing of the schoolboys about the principles of Grammar hath been continued even till our time. For I myself in my youth have yearly seen, on the eve of St. Bartholomew the Apostle, the scholars of divers [various] Grammar schools repair unto the churchyard of St. Bartholomew, the Priory, in Smithfield, where, upon a bank boarded about under a tree, some one scholar hath stepped up, and there hath opposed and answered, till he were by some better scholar overcome and put down.

In studying Thomas More—indeed, in studying all of the sixteenth century—we should never forget the importance of eloquence, learned eloquence, in the education of the young man. It is probably true that the limited number of books available in those days when Thomas More was receiving his education was an incentive to the young men to cultivate more intensely their powers of retention. The curriculum of More's school was designed to produce a young mind that could not only read and write the Latin tongue but also dispute in it.

A PAGE IN THE HOUSE OF JOHN MORTON:　　It was still the custom in More's youth for young men to go to live for some years in a household other than their own. Thomas More left St. Antony's at about age twelve to take up residence with John Morton, Archbishop of Canterbury. Morton would later become cardinal. Young Thomas More would serve in his house as page. More was to give praise to Archbishop Morton years later in *Utopia,* for in the home of and under the eye of that wise man Thomas More was to learn much. The feelings that Morton had about this young scholar were not only favorable but admiring, as is revealed in the following quotation from William Roper, More's son-in-law, who wrote what has no doubt remained the most popular life of More (however undependable it might be as a chronicle of More's life because of Roper's own particular purposes in writing it):

In whose [More's] wit and towardness the Cardinal much delighting, would often say of him [More] unto the nobles that divers times dined with him: "This child here waiting at the table, whosoever shall live to see it, will prove a marvellous man."

There is no doubting the extent of More's sophistication in the affairs of man and the world that came from his residence with Morton. The impress of the conversations that he overheard reverberated through all his later life and work.

A POOR SCHOLAR AT OXFORD: It was probably Canterbury College at Oxford that Thomas More entered after two years of residence with Archbishop Morton. More was about fourteen at the time. The rigors at Oxford were still what they had been throughout the Middle Ages. More was one of many poor scholars. About him it is said that he did not have the money at Oxford to pay for the repair of his shoes without appealing to his father. The day at Oxford began at five in the morning and did not end until ten in the evening. Totaled, there were about fifteen hours in each study day. William Roper reports that More studied both Latin and Greek at Oxford. By the time he left Oxford in 1494, More would have acquired extensive learning in the classics.

THE STUDY OF LAW: After about two years of study at Oxford, More went to London. There he was to be prepared for the life of a barrister. This move to "an Inn of Chancery called New Inn" was not a demotion for More. If he had stayed at Oxford it would have been because he was to prepare for the priesthood, "to take Holy Orders." London was the place for all young men of the time to go who were intended for accomplishment in the secular world.

More's progress in his profession by age eighteen was marked enough that he was admitted to Lincoln's Inn, and not long thereafter he was called to the Bar.

We would be wrong to think of these years of legal training as being only a tangent in More's life; his intellectual powers would, of course, continue to strengthen. It may be well for us to be reminded that these days of More's sojourn in London were days of world exploration and swelling intellectual, commercial, and religious opportunity. Besides the voyage of Columbus to the new world, John Cabot in 1497 left Bristol, England, on a voyage that would discover Newfoundland. During these London years More read in the narratives of Vespucci, lectured in the church of St. Lawrence on Augustine's *De Civitate Dei,* and listened to the numerous accounts of world travel and exploration, all influences that were to find direct expression later in *Utopia.*

A TIME OF SPIRITUAL STRUGGLE: More's father wanted him to be a lawyer. But after about three years of work as Reader in Law at Furnivall's Inn, Thomas More began to feel intensely the pressures of a deep indecision that had probably always existed, however single-mindedly he worked as student and scholar. He began a struggle over whether he would remain in the world, marry, and pursue the profession for which his study had fitted him, or enter the priesthood. The struggle would not end until some five years later when he married Jane Colt.

In order that he might have more freedom from the noise and intrusion of practical affairs, More in about 1499 removed himself to the Charterhouse of London. There "he gave himself to devotion and prayer," and lived "religiously," to use the words of William Roper, as much the life of the monks as he could. He did not take monastic vows, of course, but he entered otherwise fully into the penance and prayers of the brothers.

Thomas More was to earn his father's disapproval—even rejection. The rupture is due to the way More spent his time during those Charterhouse years. Many of More's studious hours were spent in the pursuit of mastery in Greek and in the reading of philosophy, an application of time that did not have—so the father thought—much to do with making him a good and successful lawyer. John More eventually withdrew his support of his son. Although Erasmus informs us that English law and true learning were not that closely related, we cannot forget the importance of the study of law for the life of eminence in English society at that time; a deep study of the law was necessary for a position of any considerable standing.

THE MAKING OF A HUMANIST: Before his twenty-second year Thomas More had been named by Erasmus as belonging to a company of men who were among the most famous scholars of the time: Colet, lecturer at Oxford in Paul's Epistles; Grocyn, vicar of St. Lawrence Jewry, one of More's teachers in Greek;

Linacre, lecturer in medicine at Oxford and Cambridge; and, of course, Erasmus, perhaps the most famous *humanist* scholar of them all, whose most passionate ambition was the publication of the New Testament in the original Greek with a Latin paraphrase so that the Christian could move beyond the confinements of the old Vulgate translation of the Bible and be more knowledgeable in his Faith.

We can hardly know Thomas More without knowing his *humanist* learning. But More's zealous study of Greek, the language that was to open up to man's eyes so many areas of knowledge that had been to that time locked in a strange language, did not mean that More turned against the old learning—it is in this way that he was to differ most essentially from the Protestant Reformers, those men who used the results of the new humanistic studies for showing the misunderstandings, misrepresentations, and corruptions in the existing Catholic (Universal) Church. More belonged in his most basic affinity and devotion to that body of humanists who wanted to keep the *new learning* in the service of the established, existing Catholic Church.

MORE'S SERVICE IN PARLIAMENT: More served in 1504 as a burgess in Parliament, a representative for a borough or a university; we do not know the particulars of his representation. The incident is significant for showing More's frustration of the King's purposes when Henry VII sought to exact a heavy grant of money from Parliament. William Roper tells us that Thomas More made

> such arguments and reasons there against, that the King's demands thereby were clean overthrown. So that one of the King's privy chamber, named Master Tyler, being present thereat, brought word to the King out of the Parliament house that a beardless boy had disappointed all his purpose. Whereupon the King, conceiving great indignation towards him, could not be satisfied until he had some way revenged it. And, forasmuch as he, nothing having, nothing could lose, his Grace devised a causeless quarrel against his father, keeping him in the Tower until he made him pay to him a hundred pounds fine.

The incident was an expression of that resentment of royal tyranny that comes through in a number of More's Latin epigrams from his youth. Clearly Thomas More was not to follow very closely the paths to success that his father had envisioned for him.

MORE'S MARRIAGE AND FAMILY LIFE: Colet had advised More to marry. He shrewdly recognized in the young More a predisposition to family life stronger than yearnings after the life of monastic celibacy. The account that Erasmus wrote to Ulrich von Hutten of More's devotion to his home testifies to the insight and wisdom of Colet's counsel. More's first marriage was formed with Jane Colt, and they made their home at Bucklersbury in London. Despite the objections his young, uneducated bride of seventeen made to his tutoring her, there is every reason to think that their life together was joyous. Four children were born, three daughters and a son: Margaret in 1505, Elizabeth in 1506, Cecily in 1507, John in 1508 or 1509.

More's marriage to his second wife, Alice Middleton, within the year of Jane Colt More's death in 1511 should not lead us to think that the loss of his first wife did not bring him sorrow. Our knowledge of More's life at the time clearly shows that his second marriage was formed primarily out of concern for the best interests of his children. More's marriage to Alice Middleton, a widow, did not yield to him the happiness that he had realized in his first marriage. In fact she was not sympathetic with More's concerns and involvements, and she did not possess the mind to realize the problems of the times. She was a good mother, however, and we have every reason to think that More was greatly devoted to her. A very dependable explanation for More's expedient second marriage is the amount of work he was doing at the time. The most cursory examination of the facts of More's life in 1511 will reveal an enormous expenditure of hours outside the home. In addition to his own private labor in his profession, at which he was notably prosperous, he had been made Under-Sheriff of London, an office requiring much judicial work; he was Bencher of his Inn, a post that required regular duty; he was at this time also engaged in the writing of his *History of Richard III,* a work that attacks the immoral means by which the affairs of state are administered. (If Machiavelli's *The Prince* had been printed at the time, it would be easy to read More's *Richard III* as an attack on that book.)

AN AMBASSADOR FOR MERCHANTS: The foremost of the guilds of London was the Mercers' Company. More had had a connection with that corporation since 1508. When economic relations between England and Flanders became acutely strained in 1514, his association with the Mercers in addition to his other public responsibilities made him the logical choice for a diplomatic mission to the Low Countries. Since the thirteenth century English wool had been transported to Flanders for processing into cloth. English merchants now faced the disruption of this most important source of income. The cause was the fracture of royal marriage plans—the sister of Henry VIII had been intended for marriage with the son of the Archduke of Austria, Prince Charles (afterwards Charles V). When the arrangement was broken, English resentment was expressed in a manner of dubious wisdom, namely the cancellation of the wool trade with Holland and Zealand. The English were as much punished as the reprimanded foreigners. Thomas More was chosen for the corps of diplomats who went to the Low Countries in May of 1515 to heal this economic wound. Needless to say, it was a situation requiring the most deft diplomatic touch.

More's mission to Flanders is of particular interest to the reader of *Utopia,* for it was there that More wrote Book II of the work. (Book II was written first; Book I was composed in the spring or summer of 1516.) Besides, the references that one finds at the beginning of the First Book are from the experiences of the mission to Flanders. More tells us at the beginning of Book I that the first meeting with the Flemish deputies took place in Bruges; from there they went to Brussels; having found it impossible to reach agreement on the matters at hand, they next traveled to Antwerp, where More met the exceedingly excellent Peter Giles (or Petrus Aegidius), the town clerk of Antwerp.

Although this was not the first journey to the Continent for More, his eye was probably keener for comparisons and contrasts with his home country on this stay in Bruges and Antwerp than it had been in previous travels. The differences he observed found permanent recording in *Utopia,* however much the hall of mirrors that *Utopia* is might elongate or compress reality.

MORE'S SERVICE TO HIS GOVERNMENT: More was facing another crossroads. He had been faced before with the inevitable and heavy decision whether to remain a layman or enter the clerical life. As he remained abroad for the largest part of 1515, the author of *Utopia* was pressed with the question of whether or not to give himself to full-time service to the court of Henry VIII. Henry VIII would have to look far to find a more intellectually qualified servant, but More knew, and Henry was to discover, that there were many more important considerations than the intellectual. The man who had already written passionately against the indulgent privileges granted autocratic princes would have had to have prolonged strife with the morals of the matter. The King and Cardinal Wolsey, chief minister and papal legate in England, had made efforts to persuade More to enter the royal court and its politics. Despite his frequent service to his Government, his numerous embassies, and his frequent honors, More was reluctant to be drawn into the vortex of ambition and vanity that any royal court must necessarily be. Erasmus had good reason to say of More, "No one ever strove more eagerly to gain admission there [at the royal court] than More did to avoid it."

But anyone who read More's earlier work, even the early epigrams he wrote while studying Latin, would know that his consciousness of the graft-ridden exploitation of the weak by the strong would overpower any inclination he felt to preserve private spiritual excellence in a life of restraint. More had by 1516 already seen too much of the evil results of rule by selfish and corrupt men. And there was always much room in Thomas More's heart for the underprivileged.

Further, the hope was abroad that the reign of Henry VIII would prove to be the end of tyranny in England and the beginning of a Golden Age of general enlightenment, a time for the nourishing of art, for the encouragement of deeper Christian

Faith through Church reform, for the establishment of peace. Thomas More at the accession of Henry VIII in April of 1509 cherished this hope. At the coronation of Henry some verses from More's pen spoke of "the end of bondage, the beginning of freedom," and ". . . magistracies and public offices, that were wont to be sold to bad men, [being now] freely bestowed on the good." Even after the waste of needless, pointless war, owing in great measure to the selfish interests of the vainglorious Cardinal Wolsey, men still trusted in the possibility of a Golden Age. But Wolsey had encouraged literature; in this he and More were allied. In the period of peace following the Continental wars, wars that were mostly rooted in the contest for power between Francis of France and Charles of Spain, the humanists found the occasion for renewed spirit. Erasmus, from whom we first learn of More's entering the King's service, expresses the hope of many men in the last years of the second decade:

> I see, I see, an Age truly Golden arising, if that mind of yours [Thomas Wolsey, Archbishop of York, Cardinal, Legate, Chancellor of England] should prevail with some number of our rulers. He, under whose auspices they are made, will reward your most holy efforts. And eloquence, alike in Latin and in Greek, will celebrate with eternal monuments your heart, born to help the human race.

By 1518 More was a member of the King's Council. In May of 1519 Erasmus is saying of More's life at court: "More has now become a courtier pure and simple, always with the King, of whose Council he is." Erasmus consoled himself about the loss of More from learning to royal service by saying of More that he was serving "under the best of kings."

> I should regret what has happened to More, who has been drawn into court life, were it not that under such a King, and with so many learned colleagues, it seems rather a university than a court.

Hopeful himself, but demonstrating more awareness of the brass tacks of English politics, More's comments on his new position of service to Henry VIII show more restraint:

.

Everybody knows that I didn't want to come to court, and the King often twits me about it; I sit as uneasily as a clumsy rider in the saddle. The King has a way of making every man feel that he is enoying his special favour, just as the London wives pray before the image of Our Lady by the Tower till each of them believes it is smiling upon *her*. I am not so lucky as to be a special favourite, or so optimistic as to imagine myself one. But the virtue and learning of the King increase day by day, so that I feel court life less and less of a burden.

Only a few years prior to this confession, More was carrying on a conversation in Book I of *Utopia* with Peter Giles and Raphael Hythloday about service in the king's court and the kind of life one can expect there. When More received his first money from the King on 21 June 1518 for his newly constituted position in the Government, he was receiving part of an annuity that dated from 29 September 1517. Although the next several years of More's service were to be for him a time of great success and happiness, sun-silvered clouds were soon to boil into a black tempest. One of the sounds of the coming storm was Martin Luther's hammer strokes in Wittenberg, nailing to the door of the Castle Church, Ninety-five Theses intended to encourage reform in the Church—this was on 1 November 1517.

YEARS OF DEVOTED SERVICE TO HENRY VIII: In October of 1517 More was appointed as a Judge for the Court of Requests, the "Poor Men's Court," the "Court of Poor Men's Causes," as it was known. More welcomed this opportunity for practical service to persons who had experienced misfortune and were in needy circumstances. This court dealt with matters of ownership of property, with questions of settlement in marriage, forfeiture of possessions to the King, and claims arising from injuries.

More was in Oxford in 1518, giving an address in Latin, *Letter to the Fathers and Proctors of the University of Oxford*. With particular reference to the teaching of the humanist scholar Erasmus, More gave in this address an eloquent defense of the new learning of the humanists. A contingent of the University body had come to oppose the new learning based on the study of Greek, holding the position that only the truths of the old theology were deserving of study. More not only censured the rejection of study in Greek, but he scorned as well the neglect of any area of liberal education.

The duties of a royal secretary were often carried out by More. Cardinal Wolsey maintained a continual correspondence with the persons of greatest power in European government. More would have been in touch with this network of communication. He often carried letters from Wolsey to the King and transcribed the King's replies.

One of More's services as a secretary was to participate in the composing of articles of agreement between Henry VIII and Charles, who had been elected Emperor of the Holy Roman Empire.

During the months of Henry's meetings and negotiations with Charles V, designed, of course, to establish England as a determining force in European affairs, More traveled in the King's train, serving often as a spokeman of English diplomacy in economic matters.

A certain indication of More's ascendency in royal favor was his appointment on 2 May 1521 to the office of Under-Treasurer. It may be dependable to date More's knighthood from this time. Parallels in definition and responsibility between this office and that of the Chancellor of the Exchequer have been drawn: it was therefore mainly an office for the administration of economic concern. The Under-Treasurer made each year a report to the King on a broad spectrum of financial matters, both with regard to income and expenditure.

At the same time that More's rightful place of rank and authority was firmly established in the court of Henry VIII, undertows were beginning to run beneath the waves of forceful, accomplished service to the crown. More had returned to Bruges in July of 1521 for more diplomatic talk concerning mercantile disputes. While there he was directed to join Cardinal Wolsey, who had come to France for the ostensible cause of accom-

plishing closer, more harmonious relations between Francis I
of France and Holy Roman Emperor Charles V, although it
had been considered inevitable that there would be war between them eventually. More no doubt recognized what was
evident to both Francis and Charles: Wolsey's real purpose was
to prevent a union between them, to keep either of them from
securing control over Papal power in Italy, and thereby to as-
sure the security of English power in world affairs. A year
later More was to hear Henry VIII express the ambition that
he would like to be "Governor" of France.

SPEAKER OF THE HOUSE OF COMMONS: Wolsey and
Charles V had signed an agreement in Bruges in November of
1521. After the Emperor cemented the agreement with a visit
to the English court in May of the following year, Henry VIII
made a declaration of war against France. The King found it
necessary to call for a Parliament meeting in 1523; the purpose
of the meeting was to establish policy about supplies for the
war. More served in April of that year as Speaker. In that
capacity More first faced Thomas Cromwell as an opponent.
Cromwell opposed the taxation to support the war and the plan
of an English invasion of France. Although fiercely in disagreement with Henry's foreign policy, More's loyalty to the Crown
left him no choice but to speak in support of it. Many of the
objections that Raphael Hythloday voiced in 1516 against service in royal court must have been often in More's mind during
these years.

More was meeting with agents of the Government of Francis
I in 1525. After the Treaty of Madrid between Charles V and
Francis I in January of 1526, More was working in Wolsey's
diplomatic charge toward the forming of a fresh treaty with
France. The proposal of a new matrimonial agreement between
the royal houses of England and France found More serving as
one of the signers of the treaty on 30 April 1527.

CHANCELLOR TO THE DUCHY OF LANCASTER: From July
1525 to October 1529 More occupied the office of Chancellor
of the Duchy of Lancaster. The office was one of supervision
through Duchy officials of the properties and affairs of one area
of the Kingdom's holdings, namely the inheritance of the House

of Lancaster. As Chancellor, More would have heard disputes over lands, boundaries, tolls, and disagreements in personal matters of all kinds. Around 1527 More first heard of the efforts Henry VIII was making to find grounds on which he might divorce the Queen, Catherine of Aragon, his wife since 1509. The fraudulently engineered dissolution of the marriage would bring Thomas More into a web of circumstances and charges from which he would find freedom only through a hero's death.

LORD CHANCELLOR OF ENGLAND: In order to understand Henry's causes for seeking a divorce from Catherine, we must in our own attitudes move back in history before the time when female monarchs such as Elizabeth had won fame as rulers of England. The subjects of the English Crown were not in Thomas More's time accustomed to the idea of a ruling queen. The only child that Catherine had borne Henry was a daughter, Princess Mary. Explanations for Henry's actions have included reference to the controlling importance of his establishing a male heir to the Throne.

But citations of Henry's kingly responsibility have never explained away the passion that possessed him for the vivacious Anne Boleyn, recipient of Henry's attentions—later to be recipient of Catherine's crown.

The dispensation for Henry's marriage to Catherine had been given by Julius II; Pope Clement VII would have to overrule that dispensation in order for Henry's marriage to be annulled. Wolsey travelled to France in July of 1527, accompanied by More, to seek from Francis I advice and support for the accomplishment of Henry's wish. No small part of the dilemma was that Catherine was aunt of Charles V; and Charles had sought to persuade the Pope to refuse Henry's request. A further obstruction to Henry's plans developed with the capture of Rome by Imperial troops in 1527—Clement VII came under Charles' control.

More probably had heard by the early days of 1527 the rumor of Henry's intention to divorce Catherine. During the years that he had spent at royal court in the service of his king, More had come to have great respect for Catherine; he was no doubt greatly saddened at the news of Henry's plan to divorce her after eighteen years of marriage.

In all the ensuing negotiations that Henry carried on with Clement VII, More kept silent on the question of the divorce. When Henry told More that he had discovered that his marriage to Catherine was invalid by Biblical law, and then invited More's opinion, More answered that he was "un-meet many ways to meddle with such matters." More busied himself during these months not with the King's business of divorce but with work to continue the defense of the Catholic Church from the gathering forces of Martin Luther and other Protestant reformers. He could not in good conscience help Henry end his marriage, but he could further Henry's reputation as Defender of the Faith.

Wolsey had for years been in the midst of a power struggle with Emperor Charles V and Francis I of France and had sought, with devotion and intelligence, to put England in a position of power in international affairs. As papal representative in England, Wolsey had always been able to divert Henry's concentration from the limits on kingly power in England that resulted from the power of church over state, the power of the spiritual monarch, the Pope, over the temporal monarch, the King. Wolsey's private, personal interests were involved, of course, for he had aspirations to the papal throne.

By 1527 Wolsey's position in Henry's court had become insecure. His diplomacy had fallen far short of Henry's expectations, and there was now the intensification of Henry's desire for a divorce from Catherine. Anne Boleyn was apparently prodding Henry to move against Wolsey, for she did not trust Wolsey's position on the divorce. When the Pope hesitated to grant Henry a dispensation, the blame fell on Wolsey, who was not able to bring any change in the papal position, who could not have worked that much of a change even had he wanted to. Everyone in ecclesiastical positions knew that Wolsey's fall would mean the removal of the strongest support for papal power in England.

Henry's discontent and resolve came to a focus in 1529 when

he summoned the Parliament for the purpose of initiating the separation of the English Church from the control of Rome. By 1533 this separation was so complete that Henry was able to receive a divorce from Catherine by authority of the new Archbishop of Canterbury.

Thomas More succeeded Wolsey as Lord Chancellor in October of 1529. Henry had promised More that he would not have to make either public or private agreement to Henry's intentions about the annulment or the marriage to Anne Boleyn.

MORE'S RESIGNATION AND EXECUTION: By 11 February 1531 the directions of Henry's rebellion were quite sharply drawn. A Convocation was called and, under pressures brought to bear by Henry, declared the King to be the "Supreme Head [of the Church] as far as the law of Christ allows." Henry's revolutionary move against papal power in England came at a time when religious reformation was more generally moving across the nation; the forces of the Protestant Reformation were gathering momentum at the same time Henry was diminishing the power of Rome in the Church in England.

Henry would not understand, or accept, More's opposition, although More's opposition was expressed in quiet disagreement. When Parliament in 1532 passed laws that the clergy of England be subject to the decree of the King, More resolved to resign the office of Lord Chancellor.

Henry and Anne Boleyn were married early in 1533, of course in defiance of the power of the Pope. The Act of Succession of 1534 vested the right of succession to the throne of England in the heirs of Henry and his new wife. Henry subsequently required all his subjects, not only Parliament, to swear an oath in the presence of Royal Commissioners that they would "observe and maintain" the Act; those refusing would be considered guilty of treason. More agreed to be sworn to the Succession, but he could not give his oath to that part of the document that renounced the authority of the Pope in England and that declared Henry's marriage to Catherine invalid. But More still avowed his faithfulness to Henry and his willingness to remain quiet. Henry, probably prodded by Anne, required an oath from

More, swearing acceptance of the whole Act—More would not submit to the King's wish.

In a series of shameful trials, some of the blackest stains on English history, More was ultimately convicted of treason and misprision of treason. By the decree of the recently enacted Acts of Supremacy and of Treason, More was charged with the crime of trying to undermine Henry's rule, of trying to take from the King his position and power as Supreme Head of the Church of England. Convicted on 1 July 1535 at the bar of the Court of King's Bench in Westminster Hall, More through fifteen months of imprisonment in the Tower had suffered a serious decline in health. (Any student of More's life should permit himself the moving experience of reading More's letters to his loved ones written during his imprisonment.)

In the early hours of 6 July 1536, a message was delivered to More in the Tower that he should prepare himself for death before nine o'clock that day. One must look far in the history of mankind for a more stirring example of human dignity than the spirit in which Thomas More faced his death. His courage, his faith in God, his last devotion to his friends, his triumphant humor—his adamantine stubbornness—all vouchsafe something great and magnificent about the human spirit, all speak with the fullness of tears about some essential goodness beneath the evil in the human heart, all ascribe to man a cause for life, a reason for being. To Thomas Pope More said, "I trust that we shall in heaven see each other full merrily"; to Sir Edmund Walsingham, who assisted him up the shaky scaffold, he said, "merrily, I pray you, Master Lieutenant, see me safe up, and for my coming down, let me shift for myself"; to the people gathered he said, "I call you to witness, brothers, that I die in and for the faith of the Catholic Church; the King's loyal servant, but God's first"; he knelt and repeated aloud the Fifty-first Psalm; to his executioner he said, "Pluck up thy spirits man, and be not afraid to do thine office; my neck is very short, take heed therefore thou strike not awry, for saving of thine honesty." Finally he removed his beard from the block, pushing it aside with the words, "It at least had committed no treason."

THE GENRE OF *UTOPIA*

The degree of More's seriousness is the primary issue with which we must deal if we are to arrive at a statement of what *Utopia* is as a work of literature. Did More intend *Utopia* as a handbook for officials of state, a guidebook for princes, to be read with stern attention and utterly serious purpose? Or did he intend it as a bible of truth in the matter of human relations, to be read by all sensitive men in the spirit of silent contemplation? Or, did More intend the whole work as a joke, so that we have a mere game played with a store of political knowledge and a rich imagination? Or, did More intend the work to be amusing, but to have the reader see in the ideas and events related by Raphael Hythloday (the central speaker in the work) some instructive comparisons and contrasts to his (i.e., the reader's) own conceptions of life in community with other persons?

Many critics have speculated on these questions of interpretation, and at one time or another each of these positions has been maintained. Erasmus, a famous humanist of More's time, and a friend of More's, talked of *Utopia* as if it were written as a comic book; a recent and well-informed scholar of the Renaissance has declared that there was in More at the time of writing the book the conviction that with the right kind of leadership (with the right kind of prince to head the government) England could become a utopia. The position taken by Professor C. S. Lewis in his survey of sixteenth-century non-dramatic literature is probably the most correct—*if* we keep in mind that More's purpose was a very serious one. Lewis speaks of *Utopia* as "a revel . . . [above all] of invention. . . ." Lewis says that More was writing in the spirit of debate, and paradox, in the spirit of intellectual fun.

We may in this consideration spend a moment reviewing the name of the book and the name of its central speaker. *Utopia* is by definition "nowhere"; the name More gives to the Island before it was taken over by King Utopus is *Abraxa*, which is a combination of Greek letters that have the sum (according to the numerical values given Greek letters) of 365. A heretic by the name of Basilides claimed that there were 365 heavens, and he named the most exalted of these heavens Abraxa. It is probably true that More took this name for the Island of Utopia before King Utopus became ruler, so as to suggest its mythical nature—as there was no 365th heaven, so there was no island by the name of Abraxa. (One might conjecture that More was thinking of human society in this world becoming the highest of all possible heavens, but such a line of argument would nearly have to assume that More had some reason for taking Basilides' heresy seriously—an unlikely possibility, indeed!) The name of the narrator in Utopia, Hythloday (Hythlodaeus), is constructed of two Greek words, *huthlos* and *daios*: the first Greek word means "idle talk" or "nonsense," the second "knowing" or "cunning." And so we have in Hythloday an "expert in trifles" or a character "well-learned in nonsense." Finally, the name of the river in Utopia, Anyder (Anydrus/Anydrum), is formed from Greek words meaning "waterless." It is obvious that More in writing *Utopia* is playing—but the essential question is: *What kind of game?* (Some of More's contemporaries found it difficult to know when he was kidding and when he was not.)

The best way to read *Utopia* is to think of the book as an upsidedown game, but with an ultimately serious purpose. If one considers the geography of the world of Utopia, one will realize that a line drawn from Utopia through the center of the earth to the other side would come out at the place of the globe where England is located. Think of the shape of the Island of Utopia: it is circular, and the circle in geometric lore has always been considered the most perfect figure; England, on the contrary, is shaped like a triangle, and the triangle in geometric lore is the most imperfect figure. Many such parallels of contrast may be found in *Utopia*. The most precious metal in England, gold, is used in Utopia for chamber pots; the bridge near the Capital City of Utopia does not interfere with river traffic as does the London Bridge; in Utopia there are few priests, and they are holy, whereas in England there are many who are not holy.

One genre (type) of literature in More's time was the mock oration, a kind of rhetorical exercise. In the rhetorical schools of the time the most standard literary practice was to write in praise of something in a mock way. One of the most famous of the works of this type was written by More's friend Erasmus and was titled *The Praise of Folly*. Erasmus' work was no doubt one of the stimuli that caused More to write *Utopia*. *The Praise of Folly* is a kind of learned jest, but it is not all jest: toward the end of the book Folly's oration finishes on a very serious note—the oration concludes with an indictment of worldly wisdom in the paradoxical terms that folly is wisdom, and wisdom is folly.

Thomas More's *Utopia* belongs to the same genre. It is also a learned jest. If More were writing a book of instruction for leaders of state to follow as a kind of program for founding the perfect republic, he would most likely not have euthanasia (painless death for incurables) and execution of hostile princes as practices dictated by the natural laws of the universe. *Utopia* is not either a programmatic book nor a prophetic book. *Utopia* belongs to that wealth of sixteenth-century literature that we may call mirror literature, literature written ·so that the reader may be better able to see himself as he truly is—the technique is that the reader is able to see himself in bold relief against other persons, other persons acting in situations that he may or may not actually confront himself. The purpose of a mirror is to show one's self: one may study one's flaws in a mirror. We may remember that the pastoral was one of the most popular kinds of literature in More's era. City folk wrote pastorals about country folk, because the world of country folk was a simpler world where all the motions of man are readily observable. The pastoral world is a different world—not to be desired as an actual place to live in so much as a world of contrast to the world the reader practically, concretely knows: the reader looks into the pastoral world as he looks into a mirror— to see his flaws. Let us think of Edmund Spenser's *The Faerie Queene*, a series of episodes (not organized by a unified plot) into which the young prince, for example, might look, as into a mirror, better to see himself, might look to see how he would behave in a similar situation to those in which Spenser's knights find themselves.

What More is doing in *Utopia* is making for us a mirror so that we may be able to see ourselves more clearly and more realistically. We may be able in reading *Utopia* to get outside our own world in order to get a better perspective on ourselves. More is not advocating a body of principles and laws that England should adopt, but he is thinking that his countrymen might be able in reading *Utopia* to see their weaknesses more sharply delineated. More in writing *Utopia* was not hoping for any whole reform of Christian Europe, but he did hope that some men would come to beneficial changes as a result of comparing themselves to Utopians.

PREFACE TO THE ANALYSIS AND COMMENTARY: Throughout this reader's guide the translation of *Utopia* made by Ralph Robynson in 1551 is cited both for quotation of lines and passages and for names of places. A few changes have been introduced in Robynson's phrasing where there was a possibility of confusion for the reader, and the spelling has been modernized for more expedient reading. In a number of places the alternate spellings of names and places have been introduced in parentheses.

UTOPIA

BOOK I

The inscription to Book I contains the subject of *Utopia* as a whole: "The Best State of a Commonwealth," that is, the best possible arrangement of human beings in a state or nation so that the life of each person is not only a fulfilling reality unto itself but is also a benefit to the lives of other persons.

> **COMMENT:** It is important always to bear in mind the method that More is using in presenting this study of "The Best State of a Commonwealth." *Utopia* is not to be read as a book of instructions for governors to follow. Rather, in writing *Utopia* More is putting a mirror in the hand of his reader, so that the reader can better see what he is in comparison and contrast to other men. As suggested earlier the reader of *Utopia* who is familiar with Edmund Spenser's *The Faerie Queene* may remember that Spenser tells a number of episodes in the lives of his knights so that the young courtier reading the work may compare his own behavior, actual or potential, with the behavior of Red Cross Knight, Sir Guyon, etc.

PURPOSE OF THE MISSION TO FLANDERS: At the beginning of Book I More explains his commission to Flanders at the command of Henry VIII. More's associate in the enterprise was Cuthbert Tunstal, for whose comforting companionship More gave great praise. The reason for the embassy was to discuss various aspects of the strained commercial relations of English and Flemish merchants regarding the export of English wool to Flanders for processing into cloth.

> **COMMENT:** The negotiations were to focus on such

issues as export taxes on the wool shipments and the arrangements for the sale of English cloth in the Netherlands. This embassy is the setting of the *Utopia*. But it is not the subject matter of the book; it serves only as a frame story.

More's reference to Henry as being "in all royal virtues, a prince most peerless" may serve as a reminder to the reader of the great concern in the thought and literature of More's time with the qualifications of the good ruler.

PETER GILES OF ANTWERP: When business led More to Antwerp, he had the great pleasure of meeting Peter Giles, who became to More a most perfect friend. More pays the highest compliments to him for his erudition, for his character, for his loyalty, for his sincerity. In the early paragraphs of *Utopia* More explains that Giles was responsible for relieving his loneliness for home and family.

COMMENT: More had met Peter Giles by way of an introduction from Erasmus, whom More perhaps knew by 1504. Erasmus had in reality written to Giles, asking him to give More and Tunstal any assistance possible in Antwerp. More's praise of Giles in *Utopia* for greatly diminishing his fervent desire to see home, wife, and children shows that Erasmus' request had been fully answered. More affirmed that the privilege of knowing Giles was the greatest of all his pleasures while he was traveling in the Netherlands.

MORE'S MEETING WITH RAPHAEL HYTHLODAY: By way of an introduction provided by Peter Giles, More meets Raphael Hythloday. The meeting occurs as More is returning to his lodgings from attending mass at Notre Dame. One should perhaps note carefully More's description of Hythloday:

. . . a man well stricken in age, with a black sunburned face, a long beard, and a cloak cast carelessly about his shoulders, whom by his looks and dress I judged to be a mariner.

Peter Giles tells More that Hythloday is worthy of his (More's)

time because of his (Hythloday's) own merits, not just because
he (Giles) knows him.

> **COMMENT:**   The origins of Hythloday's name are im-
> portant to note: the Greek word *huthlos* means "idle talk,"
> or "nonsense," and the Greek word *daios* may be defined
> "knowing," or "cunning." Hythlodaeus, then, would mean
> "expert in trifles," or "well-learned in nonsense." It is
> possible that More chose Raphael because the name had
> been interpreted as meaning "the healing of God": Ra-
> phael Hythloday might be thought of as an instrument of
> salvation for Christian Europe through the fantastic things
> that he tells Peter Giles and Thomas More.

Peter Giles's introduction of Hythloday to More is in these
words:

> . . . there is no man this day living, that can tell you of so
> many strange and unknown peoples, and countries, as this
> man can. And I know well that you be very desirous to
> hear of such news.

Giles carefully calls attention to Hythloday's learning in Greek.
Hythloday had studied Latin but found that the only valuable
works in Latin were certain writings by Seneca and Cicero.
Giles says Hythloday is most learned in Greek "because he had
given himself wholly to the study of philosophy."

> **COMMENT:**   More wrote to the University of Oxford
> in 1518 of the importance of the Greek language in the
> study of philosophy. More's emphasis on Hythloday's spe-
> cialization certainly reflects the humanists' concern at the
> time with the serious study of Greek.

Giles tells More of Hythloday's travels with Amerigo Vespucci,
to "know the far countries of the world." Hythloday had traveled on three such voyages and on the last had stayed behind
in the land to which he had journeyed, "as one that took more
thought and care for traveling than dying. . . ."

After More and Hythloday introduced themselves one to another, they sat down in the garden of the house where More was staying, so More informs us, and began to talk together.

> **COMMENT:** One is reminded here of the love of the Renaissance gentleman for conversation in a garden setting. At the time that More was creating the conversation in the Antwerp garden, another Renaissance personality by the name of Machiavelli was perhaps speaking to his own kind of audience in Florence.

Hythloday tells More of his adventures, how he and those who sojourned with him at the fort found friendship with the natives of that land, how they subsequently journeyed for many days and "found towns and cities and weal publics, full of people, governed by good and wholesome laws," how they went "to many countries on every side."

But More reminds us that it is not the concern of his book to tell what Hythloday said of each of his adventures, although, he says, he may recount further details of Hythloday's experiences in a later work—those, that is, that would contribute to the greater knowledge of man about how to live in community with his fellows. More clarifies that his purpose at present (in *Utopia*) is to tell what Hythloday said "of the manners, customs, laws, and ordinances of the Utopians."

> **COMMENT:** The reader should note very carefully the statement that More makes about Hythloday's accounts just before he specifies the purpose of *Utopia*. Particularly important is the use of a word that is best translated from the Latin with the English word *example*. (We remember that More wrote *Utopia* in Latin.) Observe the function of the word *example* in the following statement: ". . . so he [Hythloday] rehearsed divers [various] acts, and constitutions, whereby these our cities, nations, countries, and kingdoms may take example to amend their faults, enormities and errors."

To have an example is not the same as having a handbook of rules to follow. More is saying that the world Hythloday has seen serves as a mirror in which the English citizen—or any citizen—may look to see by comparison and contrast what he, the citizen, is, and by comparison and contrast should become.

THE DEBATE ON ROYAL COUNCILORSHIP: The introduction to *Utopia* ends at the point where More enters into debate with Hythloday on the question of why Hythloday does not take himself to the king's court and enter upon a career as royal councilor. The introduction has given an explanation of More's presence in Antwerp, it has introduced the characters, it has presented the theme of the book, it has established the tone of the work.

The principal problem with which *Utopia* grapples, namely how human beings might be able to live together in a society that integrates selfish needs into a larger whole of community welfare, is introduced in Book I with the debate over Hythloday's possible service to the royal court as councilor. Introduced also are solutions to the problem of the best state for mankind that are not really solutions; and these partial, provisional solutions, these halfway houses, anticipate the only real solution (which will be fully developed in Book II), namely brotherhood, communism, liberty—expressed in all the dimensions of human life and relationship, the political, the economic, the educational, the religious. It is in Hythloday's answers to Giles's and More's questions to him about entering the service of the king that all the possible solutions to the problem of the best state for mankind are presented: Book II will elaborate the only one of these solutions that is valid and lasting. The debate between Hythloday, Giles, and More serves really as a framework for presenting all the possible alternatives short of the communistic solution.

The transition to the debate may be said to come 1) in Hythloday's account of the skill of the mariners he had known, especially their use of the magnetic needle (one practical device, to be sure, that would contribute to the welfare of man), and 2) in More's plain statement of his purpose in *Utopia,* only to tell of the society and ways of life of the Utopians.

COMMENT: The debate that More stages in Book I may be analyzed as having three purposes: 1) to set the best state for man in bold relief against the background of states that use only partial solutions to the problem of human community; 2) to lay a groundwork for the complete structure of communistic government, which will be erected in Book II; 3) to place the reader in a setting of realistic circumstances, so that the description of *Utopia* that follows will not seem exaggerated.

FIRST ARGUMENT IN THE DEBATE: The following statement of Giles to Hythloday begins the debate on royal councilorship:

> Sure master Raphael I wonder greatly, why you get you not into some king's court. For I am sure there is no prince living, that would not be very glad of you, as a man not only able highly to delight him with your profound learning, and this your knowledge of countries, and peoples, but also meet to instruct him with examples, and help him with counsel. And thus doing, you shall bring your self in a very good case, and also be of ability to help all your friends and kinfolk.

The first argument in the debate, then, is that Hythloday by placing himself in the service of a royal court would quickly become a favorite of the king and would thereby find great fortune himself and greatly benefit family and friends.

Hythloday answers that he has already dispatched his duty toward family and friends, that he has already divided his possessions among them. Further he asserts that service to the king would really be for him a servitude that his soul finds abhorrent.

SECOND ARGUMENT IN THE DEBATE: More introduces philosophical bases for his suggestion to Hythloday that he enter royal service. Hythloday should employ his wisdom and energy for the general welfare of mankind, says More, even if he should thereby have to forego certain private liberties and pleasures. The best way that Hythloday could serve the welfare of mankind would be as councilor to some great prince (or monarch). More states as reason, "For from the prince, as from a perpetual wellspring, cometh among the people the flood of all that is good or evil." Hythloday answers More and says that the advice he would give for promoting the soundest conditions for human life in a community would be unacceptable, even if he had the ability to give such advice (which Hythloday denies that he possesses).

The first disagreement that Hythloday voices to More is that rulers find much more pleasure in contemplating the techniques and advantages of war and the methods of expanding their territorial holdings than in contemplating the conditions of peace and the means of ruling fruitfully the kingdom that is already theirs.

Further, Hythloday replies to More's logic, that a royal council is not really the setting for the honest desiring and receiving of informed advice, but operates rather as a situation for the fraudulent exchange of ambitious flattery: royal councilors give the advice that wins them the highest favor among their superiors, and the greatest political advantage in court. One of the most empty and pointless of all techniques of agreement among royal councilors to which Hythloday points is the appeal to tradition, the impeccable wisdom of one's forebears.

> **COMMENT:** Mention has already been made of the abundance of discussion in More's time of the qualifications of the prince for service to his government, whether he serves as ruler or councilor to ruler. The subject of counseling in the royal court had been at the heart of some of the best political writing in the fifty years that preceded the composition of *Utopia*. An informative parallel is chapters twenty-two and twenty-three of Machiavelli's *The Prince,* where many of the ideas on counsel current in More's time find expression.

Hythloday proceeds to stage three dramatic situations that are all designed to give graphic illustration of his reasons for refusing to enter royal councilorship. England as well as other countries come within his critical survey.

THE FIRST SITUATION: WITH JOHN CARDINAL MORTON: The first dramatic situation in illustration of his refusal to enter royal service as councilor is set by Hythloday at the table of the

Right Reverend Father, John Cardinal Morton, Archbishop of Canterbury, and Lord Chancellor of England. About Morton, Hythloday says:

> In his speech he was fine, eloquent and pithy. In the law he had profound knowledge, in wit he was incomparable, and in memory wonderful excellent. These qualities, which in him were by nature singular, he by learning and use had made perfect. The king put much trust in his counsel, the weal public also in a manner leaned unto him, when I was there. For even in the chief of his youth he was taken from school into the court, and there passed all his time in much trouble and business, being continually tumbled and tossed in the waves of divers misfortunes and adversities. And so by many and great dangers he learned the experience of the world, which so being learned cannot easily be forgotten.

> **COMMENT:** In this description of Morton by Hythloday are expressed some of the chief capacities and characteristics that are desired in a man who will serve his government. Consistently in the literature on the subject is a great emphasis on the quality of learned eloquence.

> Of course as one reads *Utopia,* one should bear in mind that the author is a man known for learned eloquence and for many years of faithful service to his government. *Utopia* is, of course, in a significant measure a presentation of Thomas More's beliefs, hopes, and frustrations. More had once written to his friend, Fisher, that he came to court only with the greatest reluctance, and that after he arrived he felt as uncomfortable as an inexperienced horseman in a saddle.

On the occasion of Hythloday's dining with Morton, there was present a layman, who was learned in English law. The layman spoke of the strict justice that was administered to thieves; they were executed by hanging, sometimes as many as twenty on one gallows.

Hythloday reports having replied to the layman that hanging

is too severe a punishment for thieves; rather, a solution should be offered by providing employment for them that would insure their being able to make a living. The main problem is not with those persons maimed in wars, for wars happen only occasionally. It is rather with the nobleman and the people he uses for his own gain. Besides the idle nobleman, and the tenants whom he exploits for all the return he can get, there is the company of idle attendants on the nobleman's ambitions, those who spend their lives in service to the nobleman, and upon his death (or upon their sickness) find themselves abandoned because they never learned a trade. Their life of service to the ambitions of a grasping nobleman has given them no preparation for manual labor.

The layman replies to Hythloday that such a lifetime of service to a nobleman should be encouraged because on it depends the strength of the army.

Hythloday replies that the layman's logic amounts to the deliberate fostering of thieves for the sake of war. Hythloday then makes reference to an even more regrettable situation in France: the French even in peacetime have established armies in residence in their country, hired mercenaries to keep the public peace. The French do not depend on novices. Consequently, Hythloday reasons, there develops a need for war so that the soldiers may have experience in their chosen profession. But, that the maintenance of standing military garrisons is unnecessary is evident, says Hythloday, in that the civilians are not afraid of the hired soldiers and can fight as well even though they have been trained to earn their living "in good crafts and laborsome works."

To the Cardinal and to the layman Hythloday names another reason for theft, the greediness of "noblemen and gentlemen, . . . and certain abbotts," who fence in all the land for pasture and leave no fields to be farmed and no places for human habitation.

Therefore that one covetous and insatiable cormorant and very plague of his native country may compass about and inclose many thousand acres of ground together within one pale or hedge, the husbandmen must be thrust out of their own, or else either by . . . fraud, or by violent oppression they be put besides it, or by wrongs and injuries they be so wearied, that they be compelled to sell all: by one means therefore or by other, either by hook or crook they must needs depart away, poor, simple, wretched souls, . . . and their whole household small in substance and much in number, as husbandry requires many hands.

COMMENT: It is obvious that Hythloday is all the time centering on the evils that come from the ambition for private property. The focus of Hythloday's censure in the above quotation is the movement for the enclosure of lands. Through the enclosure of land, fields that had been held in common are taken over by powerful individuals. Hythloday mentions two of the most conspicuous evidences of enclosure: 1) hedges to mark the area of the enclosed land; 2) the conversion of fields that had been cultivated into pasture land for sheep. The movement known as *enclosure* was discussed well into the late eighteenth century.

Hythloday tells that the greedy exploitation of the many by the powerful few necessarily brings idleness among workers, vagrancy, beggary, loss of purpose among the people, rise in the cost of food and other necessary provisions, wasting luxury, and inevitable theft. Hythloday offers the following solution:

Suffer not these rich men to buy up all, to ingross and forestall, and with their monopoly to keep the market alone as please them. Let not so many be brought up in idleness, let husbandry and tillage be restored, let clothworking be renewed, that there may be honest labors for this idle sort to pass their time in a profitable way, which hitherto either poverty hath caused to be thieves, or else now be either vagabonds, or idle serving men, and shortly will be thieves. Doubtless unless you find a remedy for these enormities, you shall in vain advance yourselves of executing justice upon felons.

After a temporary interruption from Cardinal Morton, designed to eliminate a reply by the lawyer that had all the earmarks of a piece of calculated disputation, the Cardinal asks Hythloday to give what he considers a constructive substitution for the present penalty of hanging.

Hythloday begins by saying that there is no human right or justice in making one person pay his life for another person's loss of property. The preciousness of life is all out of proportion in value to the value of any other possession. In support of his statement Hythloday cites 1) the commandment of God (one of the Ten Commandments) that no man shall take another man's life, 2) the law of Moses that the penalty for theft be a fine, not death, and 3) the logical fact that if the same punishment be administered for theft and for murder, the thief will have no legal restraint from including murder in robbery, especially so since killing the man he has robbed would eliminate a dangerous source of information about the offender.

Hythloday tells the Cardinal that the best form of punishment that he knows is that which he saw employed in the land of Persia by a community known as the Polylerites. The community is self-governing except for an annual payment to the Persian king. Hythloday reveals the following information about the Polylerites: 1) because of their geographical location at distance from the sea, their land is surrounded by mountains, and because they are so satisfied with what they produce within their own lands, they have only rare visits with other peoples; 2) they have a long-standing tradition of being content with the property they have—they do not seek expansion into other territory; 3) they are free from the needs for military expenditure because of the mountains that protect them and because of the fee that they pay to the king. After revealing these general facts about Polylerites, Hythloday comes to the matter of their treatment of thieves: 1) thieves are required to repay what they have stolen to the rightful owner, not to the prince, as is the practice in other societies; 2) thieves are subsequently placed in labor upon public works, and if they work satisfactorily they are given no further punishment; 3) they are confined at night in locked cells; 4) thieves are required to wear clothes of one color; 5) their hair is cut, but their heads are not shaved; 6) the tip is cut off their ears; 7) any gift of money to a thief is a capital offense for both thief and donor; 8) each thief wears a badge to identify himself, and it is a capital offense for him to throw the badge away; 9) thieves cannot appear beyond the bounds of their own district, nor speak with any thief from another district; 10) a thief is subjected to capital punishment if he participates in any plan for escape, whether the plan is carried out or not.

Hythloday summarizes that the purpose of all the treatment given thieves by the Polylerites is to destroy vices but to save men, to encourage such goodness in the thieves that they will live the remainder of their lives in constructive pursuits. Consequently the prisoners live in hope that they may eventually be granted liberty, and Hythloday reports that each year a number of them are granted pardon for their good behavior.

> **COMMENT:** The Polylerites have many resemblances to the Utopians that More will describe in Book II. The chief end of the life of the Polylerites as of the Utopians is personal fulfillment through shared prosperity, not the laying up of private treasures on earth through passionate seeking after luxury or fame or personal power.

Hythloday proposes the plan of the Polylerites be applied in England for thieves. The lawyer present denies the possibility of implementing such a plan in England—and, Hythloday carefully notes, everyone present agreed perfectly with the lawyer's opinion.

> **COMMENT:** More in this part of Book I is no doubt speaking through Hythloday of the ambitious courtiers who seek favor and advancement through fawning flattery of persons in power. The flattering courtiers were trenchantly analyzed by Alexander Barclay in the following lines:

> These fawning flatterers their lords thus beguile
> Yet are their lords therewith right well content
> They laugh out loud if that their lord do smile
> Whatever he sayeth they to the same assent
> And in so much are they false and fraudulent
> That if their master say that the crow is white
> They say the same, and have therein delight.

More proceeds to show how such obsequious agreement swings to the most promising position of the moment: those who had agreed with the lawyer against Hythloday readily agree with the Cardinal against the lawyer.

The Cardinal not only proposed the trial of such a plan as that of the Polylerites for the correction of thieves, but suggested it also in behalf of the vagrants in England. The whole company that had praised the lawyer's opinion now with equal zeal praised the Cardinal's plan.

At the end of his account of the experience he had at table with the Cardinal, Hythloday clarifies that his purpose was to give a case in point of the waste that it would be of himself to become a councilor to the king, where his intelligent, wisely-considered, and honestly-intended counsel would be lost in the courtiers' clamor for private power and prestige.

After thanking Hythloday for the pleasure of his story, More further encourages Hythloday to enter royal councilorship, holding still to the argument that this would be the best way for Hythloday to serve his fellow man. For further documentation of his argument More makes reference to Plato, reminding Hythloday that Plato's opinion was that only through philosophers becoming kings or kings turning to philosophy could a commonwealth be happy.

Hythloday replies to More's argument that he would be either banished or disregarded if he tried to pluck evil out of the soul of a king.

THE SECOND SITUATION: IN THE COUNCIL OF THE FRENCH KING: Here begins the second of Hythloday's dramatic situations in Book I, designed to illustrate how his salutary advice as royal councilor would be certainly met with rejection. This second situation is in the privy council of a French king.

Hythloday offers to More in example the French privy council seeking some crafty scheme whereby the French king 1) may sustain his power over Milan, 2) may restore his control in

Naples, 3) may conquer Venice, 4) may bring all of Italy under his control, 5) may rule Flanders, Brabant, and all of
Burgundy, 6) may cope with England by calling the English
nation friends but holding them in suspicion as enemies.

Hythloday asks More what would happen in such a council,
"where so many noble and wise men counsel their king only
to war," if such a simple person as himself (Hythloday) should
rise and propose quite opposite methods: 1) that Italy be left
alone, 2) that the king not enter into France, for the size of that
country meant that it could not be ruled well, 3) that he relate
to the council the decrees of the Anchorians, who live on the
southeast side of the Island of Utopia (these decrees were that
their king who had conquered another kingdom than his own
would have to choose one or the other kingdom—he would not
be permitted to retain both—for his attempt to be lord over
two kingdoms was resulting in the decay of both, 4) that he advise the French king to attend to his own kingdom and enrich
it, love his subjects and govern them peaceably.

More agrees with Hythloday that the reception given his counsel
would not be very favorable.

**THE THIRD SITUATION: IN THE COUNCIL OF AN ANONYMOUS
KING:** The third of the dramatic scenes that Hythloday
sets for explaining his resistance to royal councilorship is in the
council of an unnamed king. The councilors present are debat-
ing with the king how the royal treasury might be increased.
Hythloday names the various proposals the councilors make to
the king. One councilor suggests raising the value of money
when any funds have to be paid out and lowering the value when
expenditures must be made; another counsels a make-believe
war, for which money could be demanded from the people;
another recommends the levying of fines on those who have
transgressed certain laws that have not been for years enforced;
another advocates penalties and dispensations; another proposes
the appointment of judges who would always decide in the
king's favor, however much their decisions would bend the law.
The councilors all agree in this meeting that the king's way
cannot be in error, and that his greatest safety lies in keeping the
people poor and submissive.

Hythloday then asks what would happen if he were to arise in such a council and answer that contrary to what all these councilors have said, a king's greatest honor and safety is in the resources of his people rather than in his own treasury, that he is chosen king by the people on the basis of how well he attends to their best welfare, and therefore that he (the king) must be more attentive to their advantages than to his own; Hythloday asks what would happen if he were to say that the very name and office of king is offended by rule over subjects who live in poverty and hopelessness—if he were to declare that it is a jailor and not a king who enjoys pleasure and wealth while those around him live in deprivation and misery.

Hythloday asks further what would happen if he were to relate the law of the Macarians, a people who live not far from Utopia, the law that the king (he is so bound by an oath at his coronation) "shall never at any time have in his treasure above a thousand pounds of gold or silver."

Hythloday holds against More's arguments that his suggestions would fall on deaf ears: More agrees with him but then proceeds to clarify to Hythloday that there is an important difference between the kind of philosophy he has been propounding, school or academic philosophy, and the more fitting and effective philosophy for the practical, worldly discussions in the privy councils of kings. It is this civil philosophy that More recommends to Hythloday for his service in the government, a philosophy "which knoweth . . . her own stage, and thereafter ordering and behaving herself in the play that she hath in hand, playeth her part accordingly with comeliness, uttering nothing out of due order and fashion." More continues his advice to Hythloday in the following words:

> If evil opinions and evil persuasions cannot be utterly and quite plucked out of their [kings' and princes'] hearts, if you cannot, even as you would remedy vices, which use and custom hath confirmed: yet for this cause you must not leave and forsake the commonwealth: you must not forsake the ship in tempest, because you cannot rule and keep down the winds. No, nor you must not labor to drive

into their heads new and strange informations, which you know well shall be nothing regarded with them that be of clean contrary minds. But you must with a crafty wile and a subtle training study and endeavor yourself, as much as in you lieth, to handle the matter wittily and handsomely for the purpose, and that which you cannot turn to good, so to order it that it be not very bad.

Hythloday replies that such a method as the one More recommends seems to him a concession to the point of falsehood, a compromise of integrity: "By this means," says Hythloday, "nothing else will be brought to pass, but whiles that I go about to remedy the madness of others, I should be even as mad as they." In his reply to More, Hythloday mentions the *Republic* of Plato and the practice of the Utopians, saying that any of his listeners in such a privy council with the king would find the possibility of a state without ownership of private property strange indeed.

> **COMMENT:** In the dialogue that takes place between More and Hythloday, the issue is not one of the ethics of a man's involving himself in minor misrepresentations, but is rather that of his knowingly taking part in evil schemes that he may have later the opportunity of persuading his superiors from even worse courses of action: the essential ethical question is whether one participates in the small evil in order that one may discourage or defeat the great evil.
>
> Many critics have commented on More's indebtedness to Plato, some going so far as to say that *Utopia* is indeed a tribute to Plato.
>
> Again More mentions the Utopians. He is stimulating the reader's interest with this repeated reference to them: the references acquire added sting from the contrast that is made between the Utopians' concept of communistic sharing of possessions and the Europeans' gaining and holding private ownership.

Hythloday proceeds to tell More that he will not be like the sly and wily preachers who tailor the teachings of Christ to the corrupt ways of men. He affirms again that royal councilorship is impossible for him, because at court one will be seduced through evil company into corruption, rather than able to work reform in one's associates. It is for this reason, Hythloday says, that Plato found philosophers justified in their refusal to serve in the commonwealth.

Returning to the subject of ownership, Hythloday reveals that he cannot believe just government and flourishing prosperity to exist where there are private possessions. He cites again the Utopians, in whose society all things are held in common ownership: ". . . among them [the Utopians] with very few laws all things be so well and wealthily ordered, that virtue is had in price and estimation, and yet, all things being there common, every man hath abundance of everything."

When he thinks of the blessed state of the Utopians, Hythloday says he cannot be surprised at Plato's refusal to make laws for those who would not accept equality in the holding and sharing of goods. Plato foresaw, says Hythloday, that as "the one and only way to the wealth of a community, if equality of all things should be brought in and established." Hythloday argues "that no equal and just distribution of things can be made, nor that perfect wealth shall ever be among men, unless this propriety be exiled and banished."

More then disagrees with Hythloday, saying that the abolition of private ownership brings necessarily also the abolition of incentive: for one thing, sloth results from one man's dependence upon another man's industry, for another thing revolt comes from a needy man's not being able to retain what he has earned.

Hythloday replies to More's criticism by saying that he (More) would feel differently if he had lived with him in Utopia and prospered as he did under their "fashions and laws." Hythloday reports a five-year residence there, ending *only* because he wished to return to the world that he knew previously and share with that world what he had learned from the Utopians about the best state for human society.

After objection from Peter Giles that any country could have a better society than the one presently surrounding them, More beseeches Hythloday to tell of the land and people of Utopia, to tell in full everything about that land.

Hythloday replies that he would find nothing more pleasant, and More reports that after they had all dined, Hythloday began his account.

UTOPIA

BOOK II

Book II of *Utopia* will present the discourse of Hythloday about the Island of Utopia, its geographical arrangement, its government, its people and their hopes, beliefs, fulfillments. (The headings and subheads used below are not necessarily in the text of *Utopia* that the student will read. They are included here for his convenience in organizing the various subjects on which Hythloday speaks.)

THE GEOGRAPHY OF UTOPIA: Hythloday begins his discourse on Utopia with a description of the Island. The facts that he relates about it are: 1) the shape of the Island is like that of a new moon; 2) the island measures 200 miles across in most places, but becomes more narrow toward both ends; 3) the ends of the Island form a circle that in circumference measures 500 miles; 4) between the two ends of the Island (between the horns of the crescent) there are straits, measuring eleven miles across; 5) there is within the crescent a smooth bay, *smooth* because the land blocks off the wind: the bay serves as a harbor and accommodates convenient crossings by ships from one side to another; 6) shallows and reefs, mostly out of sight, lie beneath the water, and present a great danger to any vessel that passes through if its pilot is not familiar with the landmarks and channels; 7) a single rock of great size stands in the middle of the opening, and a garrison is built on this rock; 8) many harbors exist on the outer side of the Island, but there are such natural or man-made defenses that only a small number of defenders of the Island could keep off a large invasive force; 9) Utopia was made into an island by the conqueror of it, Utopus, who had a channel cut to separate the land of Utopia from the continent—the sea then flowed in to fill up the channel (before King Utopus came, the Island was called Abraxa);

10) there are fifty-four city-states ("large and fair cities, or shire towns," all having the same "tongue . . . manners, institutions and laws," all built alike): three wise and experienced men from each city-state meet once a year at the city of Amaurotum (at the center of the Island) to discuss matters of interest to all Utopians: because of the just distribution of property among all the people, there is no hankering after territorial expansion.

> **COMMENT:** The student should consult the Introduction, "The Genre of *Utopia*," for an anlysis of some of the names used in *Utopia*.

> Throughout *Utopia* one will find Hythloday dwelling on the many advantages to happiness and contentment of all property being held in common.

AGRICULTURE IN UTOPIA: Hythloday tells of the arrangement established among the Utopians for perpetuating fruitful agriculture: 1) a rotational plan is set up among all citizens, so that each person shares in the production of food: each citizen serves a tour of duty of two years in a rural household; a training program is established so that those who are coming to work on the farms are given instruction by someone who has already worked for a year: this arrangement eliminates any possibility of the nation's being debilitated by hunger; 2) those attending the farms are responsible to cultivate the ground, breed up the cattle, and see to a supply of wood in the city; 3) more grain and cattle are produced than the nation requires, so that the surplus may be given to the border neighbors; 4) at the time of the harvest, the citizens living in the city are informed by the magistrates, and a sufficient number of people travel to the farms to help: in this way the crops are gathered in one day or a little more.

> **COMMENT:** With regard to Hythloday's emphasis on the noble results of work on the part of every citizen, it may be illuminating to recall the idea among princes in European countries that physical labor was base and to be avoided by the élite but that effort exerted in battle or in certain sports of refinement was worthy of high regard.

An example of the deliberate element of humor in *Utopia* is More's description (through Hythloday, of course) of the hatching of eggs among Utopian farmers:

> They bring up a great multitude of pullets, and that by a marvelous policy. For the hens do not sit upon the eggs: but by keeping them in a certain equal heat they bring life into them, and hatch them. The chickens, as soon as they be come out of the shell, follow men and women instead of the hens.

Such features about *Utopia* should put the student on guard against critics who interpret the book as a serious philosophical work. There is more in the egg-hatching method, of satire, of fiction, than of a treatise on political science.

THE CITIES IN UTOPIA: After the discussion of agriculture, Hythloday comes to speak of the cities of Utopia, especially Amaurote; he chooses Amaurote as his chief example of Utopian cities because it is the one in which he lived for the five years he sojourned in the Island. (The cities, as Hythloday mentioned earlier, are as identical to *Amaurote* as the lay of the land will permit.)

About *Amaurote,* Hythloday says: 1) Amaurote is built on the side of a gently sloping hill and is measured off so that all four sides are nearly equal; 2) the breadth of the city, measuring from the crest of the hill to the River Anyder, is about two miles; 3) the length of the city, measuring along the river, is somewhat greater than the two-mile breadth; 4) a second river, which originates outside the city, is connected to the city by conduits and thereby supplies water for the city's needs; 5) around the city is a high and thick wall, equipped with towers and battlements, and with a dry, deep moat in which thorn bushes and briars grow; 6) the city has been planned so that the streets accommodate traffic easily and protect against the winds; 7) buildings are joined together in a continuous row through a block—there is no partition between them; 8) there is both a front door and a back door to each home: the doors are folding ones and are never locked—anyone may enter at any time:

"Whosoever will, may go in, for there is nothing within the houses that is private, or any man's own"; 9) the Utopians cultivate gardens with a nearly ultimate seriousness: they compete to see who can cultivate the most beautiful and the most fruitful; 10) the homes are three stories high, with flat roofs made of fire-proof plaster: windows are made of glass or linen covered with a translucent material.

> **COMMENT:** One can certainly see in Amaurote some of the characteristics of London, as More would have known London in his time. A reader of *Utopia* in the sixteenth century might see in Amaurote a mirroring of London for what it was and what it might become. If we had no evidence of his interest beyond the description of Amaurote, we would know that Thomas More yearned to see London become a clean and beautiful city. Many readers of *Utopia* have seen in More "an enlightened public health administrator."

THE RIVER ANYDER (ANYDRUM/ANYDRUS): In telling about the city of Amaurote, Hythloday relates the following facts about the chief river: 1) the River Anyder originates in a small spring located eighty miles above Amaurote; 2) the river (increased in flow by the water of several tributaries) becomes one-half mile wide by the time it flows in front of the city; 3) the water of the river reaches the ocean after a journey of sixty miles; 4) the river has alternately fresh water and salt water, according to the ebb and flow of the tide; 5) a bridge with stone supports spans the river in an area of the city farthest from the sea—this location means that ship traffic is not interfered with.

> **COMMENT:** The name of the River Anyder is made up of elements taken from the Greek language and may be defined "without water." The river, then, is "nowhere" just like the country in which it is located.

THE MAGISTRATES OF UTOPIA: Among the public servants in Utopia, there is one official known as *philarche* (in the ancient language of the Utopians this person was known as *syphograunte*) chosen by each thirty families, who is elected for a

term of one year. Over each ten *philarches* and their charges is
a *chief philarche* (*protophylarch*) (formerly known as *trani-
bore*), who serves for a period of one year. There are 200 *chief
philarches* in all.

The *philarches* choose by secret ballot a single governor out of
four persons nominated by the citizenry, one nominee from each
quarter of the city. The governor holds office for life, unless convicted of tyranny. The *chief philarches* as standard procedure
confer with the governor every day, and more often if circumstances merit extra meetings.

A decree cannot be passed without three days of discussion, an
arrangement intended to prevent tyranny and oppression. Capital punishment is enforced against any official who takes counsel
privately on matters relating to the life of the commonwealth.
Nothing is debated in the senate on the same day that it is
introduced.

OCCUPATIONS IN UTOPIA: Hythloday has previously told
how all the Utopians are trained in husbandry, how each citizen of Utopia is required to work in some form of agriculture
at specified intervals. Hythloday now clarifies that all citizens
are instructed in agriculture from the time of their childhood.

But each citizen is also instructed in some particular skill which
he can call his own. The possibilities are: 1) cloth-working in
wool or linen, 2) masonry, 3) metalworking, 4) carpentry.
(Someone in each household is expected to do the tailoring for
the entire family [all Utopians wear clothes of the same pat-
tern].) Care is taken among the Utopians to see that each person is engaged in the skills that he feels most disposed to. Most
men are trained in the skill that their fathers chose, but the
freedom to move into another specialization is granted each
citizen.

Whereas each citizen may determine how he will space out the
established six hours of work each day, no one is permitted to
be idle. Because everyone works, six hours of labor a day is
sufficient to provide the requirements of life.

COMMENT: One can feel in the tone of Hythloday's exposition about work among the Utopians that this was for More an extremely important subject. It is noteworthy that not only the necessities of life are provided through everyone's doing six hours of work a day, but the *conveniences* are provided also. A most important aspect of the presentation is Hythloday's contrast of the multitude of idle persons in other societies with the inclusive Utopian industry: he names among the idle, the professionally religious, the rich gentlemen, and noblemen, the bodyguards of noblemen, the beggars.

Hythloday's criticism takes in also the many trades in other nations that have no essential relatedness to either the necessities or the true conveniences of life, trades that produce items only for inane luxury.

The basic principles, then, in Utopian economics are: 1) everyone works, 2) the skills that the citizens perform are all useful and constructive, and 3) care is taken that no one asks for more than what is needful.

The time that remains to the Utopian citizen after he has done his six hours of labor, after periods for meals and rest, is given over to activities that will develop the mind. Daily lectures are offered in the morning for those who are interested, but the only persons who are required to attend are those who have been singled out to serve in the society as scholars. An established period of one hour's recreation is observed after the evening meal, at which time citizens entertain themselves with music or conversation. Only profitable games are permitted.

FAMILY STRUCTURE AND MUTUAL CARE:

COMMENT: Hythloday's remarks on the social structure in Utopia make the reader clearly aware that the most important element in the whole of Utopian life is the individual family. The individual family is basic to the political government of the nation, and even basic to Utopian military tactics. In this respect, *Utopia* has radically different emphasis than that of Plato's *Republic,* a work often compared to *Utopia.* Plato has no place for the family among the guardians of the state.

Hythloday begins by clarifying that "the city consists of families. . . ." Those who live in the households are usually related by blood.

In each city in Utopia there are six thousand families. There cannot be, for reasons of avoiding damaging extremes, less than ten or more than sixteen adults in each family. Persons in excess of the prescribed number for a family go to live with a family that is under the established size; families in excess of the quota in a given city move to a city that is under the quota.

Should the whole population of the Island become too large, the excess persons go to an uncultivated part of the mainland and establish a community. If the natives of the area into which they move refuse them admission to the uncultivated land, the Utopians go to war against them. On this matter Hythloday says,

> For they count this the most just cause of war, when any people holds a piece of ground void and vacant of no good nor profitable use, keeping other from the use and possession of it, which notwithstanding by the law of nature ought thereof to be nourished and relieved.

A. DISTRIBUTION OF POPULATION: In the event that the population of any of the cities falls below a number that is sufficient for its welfare (through some misfortune such as a plague), those persons occupying colonies return to the cities. The sustaining of the cities is always more important than sustaining the colonies.

B. DISTRIBUTION OF FOOD: Within the four quarters of the cities, there are storehouses. The produce of each family's labor is brought into these places, and the head of any household may come here and take away what he needs for those under his care. Nothing is refused any man because 1) there is an abundance of all needs, and 2) no one is suspected of greed.

COMMENT: Hythloday marks plainly here that pride, the chief cause in humans of excessive and ostentatious accumulation of possessions, has no place in Utopian life. Later in Book II Hythloday will say more about pride, and his later remarks are much more severe.

C. CARE OF THE SICK: There are publicly supported hospitals for the care of the sick, four hospitals for each city so that there may be no crowding and so that there may be sufficient separation of persons with contagious diseases from other patients. Because the hospitals are so well provided with equipment and capable attendants, no one wishes to remain home when one is ill.

D. COMMUNITY MEALS IN UTOPIA: The citizens of Utopia (except those eating in hospitals or those who for some special circumstance are eating in their homes) take their meals in the public dining halls especially designed and furnished for that purpose. Women do most of the work in preparation for meals, but slaves do the heaviest work. Meals begin with the reading of some materials "that pertaineth to good manners and virtue." The elders present then suggest some meaningful subject for conversation, but the younger men also participate. Music and perfumes add to the pleasantness of the setting.

JOURNEYS AND VARIOUS OTHER MATTERS:

COMMENT: In this chapter and the following one of *Utopia,* there is not the structure or order of presentation that More sustains elsewhere, for example, the excellent organization and exposition in the discussion of royal councilorship that takes place in Book I, or the chapter on war in the latter part of Book II. One may speculate that in the chapter on journeying More let his materials get out of hand, for he moves from one subject to another without logical connection or integrated transition. Consequently, in order to assist the reader in making some outline of the various subjects treated, subheads have again been introduced that do not appear in the text.

A. JOURNEYS: Continuing his account of the life in Utopia,

Hythloday explains that when a citizen desires to travel from one city to another, he appeals to the officials of his own city for permission. He is subsequently granted an arrangement for travel from the governor. But travel is not permitted without the governor's certification, and a repeated offense in this regard can condemn one to slavery.

> **COMMENT:**   Again Hythloday is careful to relate that the travelers need carry nothing with them on their journey because they find whatever provisions they need wherever they go, *since all things are held in common ownership*. But, let us note that with the privilege of receiving sustenance in any place goes the responsibility to work: should a citizen go on a journey through the area of his own city, he will not be fed until he has done his share of the work for the day.

> Attention has been directed throughout to the privileges accruing to Utopian citizens because of the communistic nature of their economic structure. Concomitantly there are Hythloday's pointed indictments of idleness.

B. SHARING OF GOODS AND TRADE: One expression of shared possessions is the ready distribution of surplus materials from a prosperous area to a deprived area without any calculation for payment or restitution.

The Utopians do carry on some export of their produce, but only after they have provided for some possibly meagre seasons in years to come. From their exports they are able to bring some needed supplies into their own country.

For the reason that they would not wish to deprive any needy people, the Utopians call in whatever money is owed them only when they must loan funds to another nation or when they must wage war. In war they use their treasury to hire professional soldiers.

C. KEEPING OF THE TREASURY: Beginning with an interesting bit of logic about how nature hides what is not useful to human creatures—gold and silver, as examples—and puts in

easy reach what is important—iron, for example—Hythloday
comes to speak of the fact that the Utopians use precious metals
for making chamber pots for all houses, for making chains for
the slaves, and as jewelry for those who are in disgrace because
of having committed some crime. "Thus by all means possible,"
says Hythloday, "they have gold and silver among them in uses
of reproach and infamy." If, therefore, gold and silver were
ever removed from Utopia no one would feel the loss.

> **COMMENT:** Hythloday tells an amusing fact about the
> use of precious stones: the Utopians use them for adorn-
> ments on little children, who when they become adults as-
> sociate such things with the state of childhood and then
> put them away as childish things.
>
> There was once a visit of Anemolian ambassadors to
> Utopia, all of whom were dressed in gold and precious
> jewels. The ambassadors fully expected in their grand
> finery to overwhelm the Utopians, but were themselves
> overwhelmed—and subdued—when the Utopians took
> them to be slaves and their servants (who were not ex-
> pensively dressed) to be masters, and when even the
> Utopian children snickered at such big children with toys.

Two of Hythloday's remarks about Utopian ideas of false and
true wealth are worth citing here:

> They marvel also that gold, which of its own nature is a
> thing so unprofitable, is now among all people in so high
> estimation, that man himself, by whom, yea and for the
> use of whom it is so much set by, so highly regarded, is in
> much less estimation, than the gold itself.
>
> But they much more marvel at and detest the madness of
> them, which to those rich men, in whose debt and danger
> they be not, do give almost divine honors, for none other
> consideration, but because they be rich: and yet knowing
> them to be such mean and miserly persons, that they be
> sure as long as they live, not the worth of one farthing of
> that heap of gold shall come to them.

D. STUDIES OF THE UTOPIANS: Other than those who are singled out for a life of scholarship, many persons devote their hours of leisure to learning. Children are brought into contact with good literature from an early age.

The Utopians study the several areas of human knowledge in their own language, which has a large supply of words, a pleasant sound, and a facile syntax.

Hythloday tells that the Utopians when he found them 1) knew nothing of the famous philosophers, 2) were not qualified to compete in modern logic, 3) did not speculate about the arrangement of heavenly bodies. But he found that they 1) had made very nearly the same discoveries as the classical scholars had made in music, logic (dialectic), arithmetic, and geometry, 2) had become most knowledgeable in the movement of heavenly bodies—even to the point of developing astronomical instruments, 3) had discovered means of forecasting weather, 4) had learned to dispute in philosophy as other men do.

E. PHILOSOPHY OF THE UTOPIANS: The Utopians include in their philosophy 1) inquiry into the nature of the good, 2) inquiry about the soul, body, and faculties of man, 3) discussion about virtue and pleasure, 4) most significantly to them, consideration of what constitutes happiness. (Hythloday says with regard to the question of happiness that the Utopians make pleasure more the determining factor of happiness than he thinks they should.)

F. THE UTOPIAN CONCEPT OF PLEASURE: The Utopians support their doctrine of pleasure as the greatest happiness with theological bases. Positing belief in immortality, the Utopians hold that there is reward for virtue and punishment for crime in the afterlife.

Man possesses reason, and this capacity in him disposes him to virtue; the virtuous act leads man to pleasure and therefore to happiness—the logic is that God created man for virtue and therefore for pleasure and therefore for happiness. The only thing that dissuades man from a pleasant course of action is the capacity for virtue in him that leads him to a *greater* pleasure.

One is rewarded with happiness in the afterlife for pursuing the greatest pleasure in mortal life. Our reason directs us to seek pleasure; to follow the dictates of reason is virtue.

Further, it would not be virtuous to disregard another's pleasure, for to do so would ultimately be the course of lesser pleasure for the disregardful person. "For it [the practice of regarding another's pleasure]," says Hythloday on this subject, "is recompensed with the return of benefits; and the consciousness of the good deed." "Finally . . . God recompenseth the gift of a short and small pleasure with great and everlasting joy."

There is a class of pleasures that is spurious, even though those spurious pleasures are the ones to which man is led through distortions in his reason. Hythloday says the Utopians include among the spurious pleasures the wearing of expensive garments, or the claiming of honor for being born into a moneyed heritage, or the accumulating of jewels, or the laying up of wealth. What true pleasure can come from these, he asks, when they are all external to a person's real needs and longings.

> **COMMENT:** One can feel in *Utopia* and elsewhere in More's works that he considered reason and faith to be complementary powers: the reason of philosophical inquiry and faith in the divine revelation of God cooperate in helping man find the meaning of his existence.
>
> One of Hythloday's criticisms of wealth is that what it is in its very nature nearly necessarily means that it is superfluous, that is, not invested for definitely fruitful return for man. Wealth, then, is a kind of decoration, and as such is a false pleasure.

Hythloday tells that the Utopians also regard the following as false pleasures: playing with dice, and hunting and hawking. The only persons who hunt in Utopia are slaves who do the work of butchering animals for food—hunting is "a thing unworthy . . . of free men." The hunter's pleasure in killing any kind of beast could only come from a cruel disposition, and as a practice could only result in a worse cruelty in the mind of hunter. Such pleasure in bloodshed could occur only because the essentially good nature of man had become perverted: disease or habit can be perverting forces.

The Utopians think that genuine pleasures come from both soul and body. Pleasure in the soul comes from intelligence, "the contemplation of truth," memory of a fruitful life, and hope in human happiness. There are two kinds of bodily pleasure: pleasure from the natural physiological processes—rest, refreshment in food and drink, sexual intercourse, elimination, the titillation of certain sensations like music. The second kind of bodily pleasure—to the majority of Utopians the very basis of all other pleasures—is that of a good state of health, which the Utopians say man is indeed able to feel in his normal round of activities.

At the top of the hierarchy of pleasures the Utopians place the pleasures of the mind, "the chief and most principal of all": these pleasures derive particularly from "the exercise of virtue, and consciousness of good life."

The Utopians, Hythloday is careful to clarify, do not appreciate a pleasure of the body just for itself, for they reason that if a man were to find great pleasure in scratching as a pleasure that was an end in itself, then he would go on itching forever. They understand, rather, that the pleasure must be more deeply related to the whole state of man's health and well-being.

In whatever pleasures the Utopians participate, they always hold to the basic principle that attention should not ever be diverted away from the greater genuine pleasure through attention to the smaller spurious pleasure.

Hythloday concludes his revelations about the Utopian concepts of pleasure with supportive evidence of the accuracy and soundness of their views and behavior. One need not argue about whether the Utopians are right in their ideas or not, one need only look at the evidence: 1) the nation is a happy one, 2) the people are healthy, active, strong, and suffer few diseases, 3) they make the most of their disadvantages, 4) they have plenteous supplies, 5) they are people of pleasant disposition, and ingenuity, 6) they work cheerfully, 7) they study diligently.

G. INTELLECTUAL GIFTS AND ACCOMPLISHMENTS OF THE UTOPIANS:

Hythloday recounts the efforts he and his companions made to share some of their learning with the Utopians, owing to the great interest that the Utopians showed in the Greek learning of their guests. Hythloday and his company were amazed at the rapid progress the Utopians made, and Hythloday speculates that the precocity of the Utopians in their study of Greek language and literature was in a measure because they were of Greek derivation.

Of the writers that the Utopians had come to possess when he visited there, Hythloday names Plato, Aristotle, Theophrastus, Lascaris, Hesychius and Dioscorides. Especially did the Utopians show interest in Hippocrates and Galen (both classical writers on the subject of medicine); to these two writers the Utopians assigned great value. Although the Utopians do not particularly need instruction in the arts of medicine because of their remarkable freedom from illness, they still regard medicine as one of the most important branches of philosophical inquiry. Hythloday's explanation of the reason for this phenomenon of interest is as follows:

> For while they by the help of this philosophie [the science of medicine] search out the secret mysteries of nature, they think themselves to receive thereby not only wonderful great pleasure, but also to obtain great thanks and favour of the author and maker thereof. Whom they think, according to the fashion of other artificers, to have set forth the marvelous and gorgeous frame of the world for man with great affection intentively to behold.

Revealing of the multitude of the Utopians' interests is the energetic welcome they give to persons coming to their land from other places who have any particular command of an area of knowledge or any particular information about other lands and other peoples.

> COMMENT: One important evidence of the kind of Christian humanism that penetrates More's thought is that the scientific investigations carried on by the Utopians are oriented within their faith in God: they praise God by studying His universe.

SLAVERY, THE SICK, MARRIAGE, LAW:

A. SLAVERY: Slaves in Utopia include: 1) prisoners of war from other countries with whom the Utopians have themselves carried on war, 2) Utopians guilty of very serious crimes, 3) persons who have been sentenced to death in other countries but bought from that country by Utopians, 4) refugees from other countries who prefer slavery in Utopia to the kind of life they previously had.

> **COMMENT:**   The slaves in Utopia do not form a separate and distinct social stratum. Slavery in Utopia is not passed on within a family from one generation to another: it is not hereditary in character. Slavery in Greece and Rome had been established for a class of people. Servitude in Utopia for Utopian citizens is mainly for crimes they have committed.
>
> Slavery in Utopia is mainly a matter of work. In their shackles of gold and silver, the slaves farm, butcher, work in the dining halls, hunt for food, and do various kinds of work in connection with the maintenance of public works.

B. THE SICK: Hythloday earlier in his account of life in Utopia to Thomas More and Peter Giles told how lovingly and exactly the sick are cared for. He adds now more details, including the way those persons incurably ill are counseled by the priests and public officials to euthanasia, accomplished either by starvation or by being put to sleep: but euthanasia is not practiced on any unwilling person.

> **COMMENT:**   In this statement about the care of the sick, More gives through Hythloday the most favorable expression about priesthood in the whole of the work.
>
> The drug used to bring about death could be *mandragora,* mentioned by Erasmus. Or, it could be *hemlock,* drunk by Socrates.

C. MARRIAGE AND DIVORCE: Minimum ages for marriage in Utopia: women—18; men—22. Persons participating in premarital intercourse are severely punished, and the parents in whose dwelling the sexual relations took place are held in disgrace for their carelessness in supervision. The reason for Utopian strictness in the matter of premarital sexual relations is that this indulgence is considered damaging to persons' interest in marriage.

Before marriage both man and woman are submitted to visual examination by the other. In the presence of guardians both the young woman and the young man who are intending marriage are brought naked into each other's presence. This way the Utopians eliminate one important source of marital dissonance, for they recognize the importance in marriage of mutual pleasure in the body.

One of the reasons for such care about marriage is that customarily death is the only end of the relationship between man and woman. Adultery or *extreme* repugnance are the only other grounds for divorce. Divorce and remarriage must occur under the supervision of officials in the government. Adultery is punished by slavery. If the marriage is reconstituted, a second occurrence of adultery brings the death penalty to the offender.

D. EXERCISE OF OTHER LAWS IN UTOPIA: No definite penalty exists for crimes, generally; a body of public officials decide on the penalty according to the nature of the crime. For the most part, slavery is a preferred penalty, since slavery can have a benefit for the state, and since the punishment of slavery can serve longer as an example to the other citizens. But insubordinate slaves are executed. Pardon, however, is possible. Tempting another to crime is as serious an offense as committing the crime.

Men are rewarded for virtuous deeds, one example of which is the erection of statues in the marketplaces.

Any man who goes out and canvasses for votes is eliminated from any chance of holding office.

Any lawyer in the Utopian society who is discovered in any kind of dishonesty or destructively crafty interpretation or application of laws is banished. In fact, every citizen is asked to speak as his own defense lawyer: this procedure, the Utopian feels, leads to the greater truth.

The Utopians keep very few laws, and they criticize other societies for having so many. Each citizen is expected to be fully informed of the meaning and administration of the laws that exist.

The basic concept of the law in the Utopian scheme of things is that the law is to remind the citizens of their rightful responsibility. An important consequence of this concept is that the plainer interpretation of the law is the more just.

The excellence of the Utopians in the implementation of legal justice has caused surrounding societies to seek officials for their governments from Utopia, knowing, as they do, that the prosperity or failure of a commonwealth depends on the character of the men governing it. The two qualities that can most be depended on in the Utopians are freedom from favoritism and freedom from avarice.

The Utopians do not make treaties with other nations, for they have often seen how treaties agreed on between other nations were too soon broken. The Utopians rely on their inner integrity to vouchsafe the inviolability of any treaty they form. The natural value of basic human quality, and that quality expressed in relationships, the Utopians consider the most valid bond of agreements between nations: words written into a signed and sealed document will not add to that value.

> **COMMENT:** More uses the opportunity of Hythloday's remarks on treaties to speak at some length through him of the lack of basic trust among men, as the deficiency finds expression in the deceit and camouflage of international relations.

> But in that new found part of the world, which is scarcely so far from us beyond the line equinotical, as our life and manners be dissident from theirs, no trust nor confidence is in treaties. But the more and holier

ceremonies the treaties is knit up with, the sooner it is broken by some cavilation found in the words, which many times of purpose be so craftily put in and placed, that the bands can never be so sure nor strong, but they will find some hole open to creep out at, and to break both league and truth.

WARFARE AS THE UTOPIANS UNDERSTAND IT AND PRACTICE IT:

COMMENT: This chapter of *Utopia* more than several others is logically developed and structured in a unified way. One may with considerable ease outline it in three rather distinct sections: 1) the reasons for warfare, 2) the techniques of battle, 3) the signing of truces and the settling of accounts.

A. REASONS FOR WARFARE: First of all, the Utopians detest war, and Hythloday seems to say that they are shocked that man is so often involved in it. In line with their basic abhorrence is the feeling that Hythloday attributes to them in his statement, "they count nothing so much against glory, as glory gotten in war."

But, the Utopians will go to war for the following causes, and they are causes of the most grave importance: 1) to defend their own country against invasion, 2) to defend the property of a friend from invasion, 3) to deliver an oppressed people from tyranny, 4) to avenge their friends on an adversary who has wronged them (i.e., their friends), 5) to avenge the malicious injury or murder of one of their own citizens if the guilty parties within a nation are not handed over to them for punishment. (The Utopians demand, however, that they be consulted before the wronged nation takes retaliatory action.)

COMMENT: For all of their reasons for going to war with other nations, interestingly the Utopians do not avenge themselves on any nation that has caused injury to them: in such an instance, when, say, they have been cheated in trade, they only withdraw from further commerce with that nation until restitution has been made.

The cause at the heart of this restraint is their communistic economy. Expressing again the central importance of public ownership of property in Utopia, Hythloday explains that the reason the Utopians do not go into war to avenge themselves on whatever nation has wronged them in commerce but do go to war when nations friendly to them are wronged is that in Utopia no injury comes to individuals through such fraud in commerce, since only that produce superfluous to their needs and conveniences is expected, whereas in other nations that have private ownership of property, individuals are hurt by the loss. It seems cruel to the Utopians for any nation to cause suffering and death to many persons in war when actually their own citizens have not been *individually* hurt.

B. TECHNIQUES IN WARFARE: The Utopians are most jubilant in victory when they have won over their adversaries "by craft and deceit," that is, by stratagem and cunning. They make the greatest claim to valor and heroism if they have defeated their enemy through the power of thought rather than through the power of arms.

For with bodily strength (say they) bears, lions, boars, wolves, dogs and other wild beasts do fight. And as the most part of them do pass us in strength and fierce courage, so in wit and reason we be much stronger than they all.

1. At the beginning of any war, the Utopians dispatch persons secretly to go into enemy territory and place in conspicuous locations proclamations bearing their own seal, proclamations that offer great rewards to anyone who will kill the king of the nation they are attacking. They offer rewards also for the murder of lesser powers in the enemy government. A double recompense plus personal safety is offered to any of the persons named on the proclamations who turn traitors, or to any man who turns over one of these persons to them (i.e. to the Utopians).

COMMENT: Thomas More is no doubt using this opportunity to comment (through his character, Hythloday) on the general untrustworthiness of men in positions of power (including kings!). Hythloday tells of the immediate treachery that develops after this publication of notice of wanted persons:

> Therefore it quickly comes to pass that their enemies have all other men in suspicion, and be unfaithful and mistrusting among themselves one to another, living in great fear, and in no less jeopardy. For it is well known, that divers [various] times the most part of them (and especially the prince himself) hath been betrayed of them, in whom they put their most hope and trust. So that there is no manner of act nor deed that gifts and rewards do not enforce men unto.

It is hardly necessary for the reader to be reminded of the passionate concern in a great part of sixteenth-century English literature with the question of the qualifications and training of the young prince, the young man who will devote his life to the service of the government. Here, in this part of More's discussion of techniques of war is a mirror for the prince to look into; here is the behavior of other princes put on display so that the reader may see himself more clearly.

The student may wish to compare two other famous sixteenth-century works when reading *Utopia* as a mirror work: George Gascoigne's *The Steel Glass,* and the very famous work of the Elizabethan period, *A Mirror for Magistrates.*

The rationale of the Utopian scheme for seducing their enemies to treason is that the fewer people who suffer in war, the better—"by this means [they] dispatch great wars without any battle or skirmish." By putting to death a very small number of persons in the enemy government, the Utopians protect from injury and death many innocent persons—both among their own citizens and among the foreign people: the Utopians are concerned about both.

2. Another of the Utopian techniques for bringing any war to an end without shedding of blood and loss of life is to incite com-

petition for the throne among persons in positions of power in the alien government, for example, the brother of the king or noblemen.

> **COMMENT:** The mirror again! One may think of this as education for the public servant through representation. It is not information through stated principles or rules, but information through example, the kind of instruction one gets just by watching other humans in action (this is the kind that lasts, too).

3. A third technique that the Utopians use in war is to remind the peoples who live around their enemy of some old territorial dispute.

4. The Utopians readily use the funds they have held in reserve (one remembers that they keep their gold and silver for this purpose) for hiring mercenaries to fight their battles for them, if the conflict comes to require such aggression. The Utopians are always eager to preserve each other from injury. Mercenaries are drawn especially from the Zapoletes (Zapoletans), who live eastward from the Island of Utopia at a distance of 500 miles; they are a people known for their endurance and aggressiveness, a people that lives by hunting and plundering: "They be born only to war, which they diligently and earnestly seek for." The Zapoletes learn no other trade than fighting. They love fighting so much that they offer their services for a very low fee; but they will change their allegiance immediately if they are offered a higher wage by the army they are fighting against— they have no allegiance to any cause or principle.

> **COMMENT:** When Hythloday speaks at considerable length on some aspect of Utopian life, one can assume that Thomas More's voice is breaking through on some issue of particular importance to him. With regard to the Zapoletes, Hythloday tells us much more than we need to know in order to be aware of how the Utopians hire mercenary soldiers.
>
> The heat of More's own thought seems especially focused here on the ugly human fact that men related to

each other in blood will destroy each other for a few pennies. Again we have an indictment of the evils of private enterprise: the experience of the Zapoletes shows that the promise of making a little more money destroys families, turns loved ones against loved ones, is generally destructive of the most precious realities of human life.

The Zapoletes fight in the service of the Utopians against any adversary, simply because the Utopians pay them more. Because of the character of the Zapoletes and the savage kind of life they live, the Utopians do not try to protect them from destruction. In fact, the Utopians would feel that they had done the human race a great service if they were instrumental in the utter destruction of the Zapoletes. "For the Utopians like as they seek good men to use well, so they seek these evil and vicious men to abuse."

Besides the Zapoletes, the Utopians engage troops from the nation for whom they are going to war.

5. The last soldiers added to the total fighting force are Utopian citizens, and from among these are chosen the commanding officers. Those of the Utopians who fight are volunteers, and never is anyone forced to fight against his will. The Utopians try always to avoid putting their own citizens into battle; they depend on outside sources for as much of the army as they can.

6. Wives may accompany their husbands into battle, and families stand together in actual combat. Because those who are related to each other in the most binding of human relationships stand side-by-side in battle, wars can be long and casualties heavy. When forced to it, the Utopians are indeed fierce on the battlefield, moreso, obviously, since their energies are not divided with worry about home and family.

7. It is characteristic of the Utopian style of fighting that they begin with a less aggressive effort and build into a ferocious one.

8. Another stratagem that the Utopians employ is that of dis-

patching a body of carefully chosen young men to seek out and destroy the enemy captain. This they accomplish by open assault or covert ambush.

9. A standard practice among the Utopians in battle is not to pursue a retreating army, for they have several times when being routed turned on their enemy and in the midst of their enemy's jubilation and relaxed defenses turned a loss into a victory—they do not wish to risk having the same experience.

10. Through engaging the efforts of every soldier who is not on guard duty, the Utopians quickly build strong fortifications, one of the most important of which is a ditch dug around their camp.

11. The armor the Utopians use is very sturdy, rugged enough to endure any blows their enemies inflict, but flexible enough that, for example, the Utopians can swim with it on. (Weapons used by the Utopians include many ingenious devices beyond the standard weapons of arrows and battle-axes.)

12. The Utopians are prepared for any warfare into which they might be forced to enter. Besides their particular training, they are supported by their basic attitudes toward life given them by their excellent instruction and by the influences of the institutions among which they grow and mature. Hythloday summarizes the results of their training and influences in the following words:

> By reason whereof [their training and influences] they neither set so little store by their lives, that they will rashly and unadvisedly cast them away: nor they be not so far in lewd and fond love therewith, that they will shamefully covet to keep them, when honesty bids leave them.

13. There is also among the Utopians a marvelous flexibility with respect to their advance and retreat tactics. They do not press the fight when they have wisely determined that theirs is the weaker situation or the disadvantage. The heroic spirit of the Utopians does not get in the way of the clever strategy they use—they do not go to war to be heroes but to win! This basic

flexibility serves the purpose also of keeping their enemy off guard: the enemy can never determine what the Utopians are about to do.

C. SIGNING TRUCES AND SETTLING ACCOUNTS: The Utopians avoid carnage after battle, and they take prisoners alive. The cities and fields of the enemy are left as much unharmed as the Utopians can permit; they do not ravage cities or burn fields.

The expenses of the war the Utopians charge to the conquered, not to the nation for which as friends they have gone to battle. They ask the conquered nation for money as is necessary, and then they take over estates in the conquered nation for future revenue.

> **COMMENT:**   With regard to Utopian behavior in the aftermath of war, we find another stricture against private property in Utopia. No Utopian is permitted any booty from a victorious battle. Whatever materials are confiscated from the enemy are turned over to the nation whom the Utopians have avenged. Monies are never hoarded: funds are left in circulation in the economy of any conquered nation until the Utopians have need for them.

The Utopians keep any truce they have made with a religious kind of zeal.

RELIGION IN UTOPIA:

A. MANY RELIGIONS BUT ONE GOD: The Utopians permit a variety of religions among their people. Some worship the sun as God, some the moon, some the planets they see in the heavens, some virtuous and glorious men of the past. The greatest number of the citizens, however, hold to a faith in one God, "unknown, everlasting, incomprehensible, inexplicable. . . ." This majority recognizes the one God as *Father,* and they believe that He expresses His power and virtue throughout creation. "To Him alone," Hythloday explains, "they attribute the beginnings, the increasings, the proceedings, the changes and

ends of all things." Even those persons who cannot ascribe such sovereignty, such providence to one God, and who orient their worship toward stars or planets or famous men, still acknowledge the existence and ultimate control to one supreme Being, "to whose only divine might and majesty, the sum and sovereignty of all things by the consent of all people is attributed and given."

Hythloday reports a current trend among Utopians to move away from the many different beliefs they have held (a "variety of superstitions," he calls them) and come to one united belief that seems the most reasonable of all the beliefs. Hythloday speculates that this concord of religious conviction would have occurred earlier had it not been that a person considering a change in his religious faith interpreted an event as a divine warning sent to him.

B. THE UTOPIAN RECEPTION OF CHRISTIANITY: Hythloday speaks of the eager reception the Utopians gave to the Christian Faith; many persons upon hearing of the life and ministry of Christ and of the martyrdom among the followers of Christ for the defense of their faith wished to become Christians. Hythloday thinks that one of the most persuasive facts about the Christian Faith to the Utopians was its active implementation in the actual everyday life of believers.

The Utopians who accepted Jesus Christ as Lord were given all reception into the Christian Faith except for the administration of the sacraments, which could not be offered because there was no priest in Hythloday's company.

C. RELIGIOUS FREEDOM AND TOLERATION AMONG THE UTOPIANS: The natural generosity of spirit among the Utopians was evident in the fact that those who did not accept the Christian Faith did not try to keep others from accepting it. The only incident of censorship came from a newly baptized Christian who immediately took up evangelical cudgels against his people, condemning the other Utopians to everlasting damnation for not becoming Christians. He was subsequently banished.

COMMENT: The sentence of exile for this violent

preacher demonstrates how much value the Utopians set by the freedom of religious belief and religious worship: "For this is one of the most ancient laws among them," Hythloday clarifies, "that no man shall be blamed for reasoning in the maintenance of his own religion."

Banishment or slavery is the customary sentence applied to persons found guilty of *inordinately zealous proselytizing*. Any person is free to express his faith, and free also to persuade others to take up his beliefs—but it has been the practice in Utopia from the beginning of the present nation to permit persuasion only through sane reasoning: no one is permitted to become loud and abusive if any other person disagrees with him. This principle of religious freedom and toleration was established at the very beginning of the nation by King Utopus, the founder of Utopian society in its present state. Utopus was thinking of the preservation of peace when he passed legislation about freedom in religious thought and expression. But another of his chief concerns was that he was not sure that God did not Himself desire different forms of worship: it was possible, Utopus reasoned, that God actually Himself inspired man to a variety of religious expression.

King Utopus held two basic convictions about religious faith and its articulation: 1) it could only be foolish and destructive for any man through means of violence and coercion to bring another man to the acceptance of some position; 2) the truth about religious faith would ultimately triumph, whatever imperfect forms of religious expression existed in the intervening time. But, if truth will eventually triumph, the worst of men will be the most unyielding in the interim time: King Utopus reasoned that bringing decision about religion to the level of combat would mean the defeat of the holier position.

King Utopus placed only two restrictions upon religious faith and practice in Utopia. The Utopians regard any man as subhuman if he believes either 1) that the soul dies when the body dies, or 2) that life in this universe is merely a thing of capricious chance. King Utopus further required the citizens of Utopia to believe that there was reward for goodness and punishment for evil in the afterlife.

But there is no specific punishment for a nonbeliever, primarily because the Utopians believe that such inhuman ideas in his mind will eventually be replaced by reason. The nonbeliever, however, is permitted to hold no office and is given no public function or public honor; further, he cannot express his beliefs in the presence of other citizens unless those citizens are priests.

D. UTOPIAN IDEAS ABOUT DEATH AND BURIAL:

> **COMMENT:** If the reader of *Utopia* has any background in the literature of the Old and New Testaments (Biblical literature), and any knowledge of the history of the Christian Church and its present practices, he may wish to make comparisons throughout this chapter on religious thought and life among the Utopians. A more fruitful way of reading this part of *Utopia* than thinking of it as More's body of doctrine for Christian Europe would be to ask what light the Utopian beliefs and practices shed on faith and conduct in Western Christendom.

The Utopians lament the death of any citizen who seems to depart from mortal existence with fear and reluctance. They think that this kind of resistance to death reveals some awareness in the human soul of guilt and imminent punishment. Such a person is given a solemn funeral and is buried.

The Utopians rejoice in cheerful deaths, and joyful funerals are observed for those who depart cheerfully from mortal life, and their physical remains are cremated rather than buried. The merits of the deceased person are engraved on a pillar that is erected at the place where the cremation has taken place. Besides serving as a fitting farewell celebration for the dead, the Utopians think that establishing such a memorial is a good example to the living.

> **COMMENT:** In another of his works, namely his work on Christian eschatology ("Last Things"), More interprets the concern of a dying man for funeral plans to be a temptation from the devil. More says that at such a time,
>
> instead of sorrow for our sins and care of heaven, he

[the devil] puts us in mind of provision for some honorable burying, so many torches, so many tapers, so many black gowns, so many merry mourners laughing under black hoods, and a gay hearse, with the delight of goodly and honorable funerals: in which the foolish sick man is sometime occupied, as though he thought that he should stand in a window, and see how worshipfully he shall be brought to church.

For an interesting modern comparison to Utopian attitudes, the student may wish to read "Tract," by the American poet, William Carlos Williams, a poem of seventy lines in which Williams addresses himself to the folk of his home town, Rutherford, New Jersey, about their funeral customs.

Among the Utopian beliefs about the afterlife is the trust that the souls of departed ones are present when mortals speak of them. Such a confidence is only logical, for it would be inconsistent with the blessedness of afterlife to think either 1) that the immortal did not have greater freedom of movement than the mortal, or 2) that the departed souls did not wish to return to visit their friends on earth. The Utopians believe freedom to be increased after death rather than diminished, like all other gifts to which good men may look forward.

E. MIRACLES AND MAGIC: Whereas the Utopians believe in miracles—obvious disruptions of natural processes by divine power—they hold in derision such superstitions as soothsaying and auguries read in the flights of birds.

F. SOME FORMS OF WORSHIP OUTSIDE WORSHIP SERVICES: Labor invested in the study of natural phenomena or the physical laws of the universe the Utopians credit as worship of God.

But some persons prefer to work for the rewards of the afterlife through physical labor such as nursing the sick, repairing roads, working as servants. No one is reluctant in Utopia to spend his life as a slave for reason of fearing derision from his fellow citizens: volunteer slaves are highly regarded in Utopia.

1. ASCETIC SLAVES: One class of slaves in Utopia are religious ascetics. Rejecting the pleasures of the mortal life as harmful, they abstain from sexual relations and from eating flesh: they occupy their hours on earth with eager watching for the afterlife.

2. "WORLDLY" SLAVES: A second class of slaves participate in marriage, beget children, eat meat, do hard labor, and permit themselves any pleasure that does not prove an interference with the work they elect to do.

Utopian society considers the second kind of slaves the more sane of the two, but because the first class, the ascetic slaves, give religious reasons for their behavior, they are considered the holier.

The first class of slaves is called Buthrescas.

G. THE UTOPIAN PRIESTHOOD: A maximum of thirteen priests serve an equal number of churches in each Utopian city. There is no larger number than thirteen permitted because the Utopian priests are of such sterling character, and, too, this limitation of number helps to preserve the excellence and dignity of the office. The priests are elected by a secret ballot taken from among the people.

The functions of the priesthood include 1) the supervision of worship services, 2) the exercise of moral discipline among the people, 3) the provision of counsel for the people, 4) the supervision of the education of the youth.

Women may be elected priests, but only a widow of considerable age is ever chosen and then only rarely.

Owing to the extremely exalted virtue of those persons elected to the priesthood, and the extremely high regard in which the office of priest is held, no priest is ever subjected to penalty or punishment for wrongdoing: he or she is merely left to the disciplinary handling of God.

The Utopian priests are respected among all nations, not only among their own. The priests have won great respect by actually appearing near the scene of battle during wartime and praying for peace. Although they direct their prayers first of all for victory for their own side, their prayers include a plea for delivery of all the people from injury and death. A demonstration of their true generosity is in their efforts to restrain the men of their own side from doing harm to the soldiers of the routed adversary. They intercede also in the name of peace and avert any carnage that might come from a conquering army in the high spirits of victory.

H. HOLY DAYS AND WORSHIP SERVICES: The first and last day of each month and the first and last day of each year are established as holy days. First days are called *Cynemernes (Cynemerni/Lynemernes),* and last days *Trapermernes (Trapemerni/Trapemernes).*

The architecture of Utopian temples is splendid, and the temples are large enough to accommodate a multitude of worshippers. Further, to benefit the concentration of the worshippers, dim light is used in the temples rather than bright light.

The temples are not furnished with symbols or statuary that would inhibit any person in his worship, whatever form that worship takes: any furnishings that appear have been given a careful scrutiny so that they do not interfere with any one's faith or devotional habits in worship services. All prayers are spoken with the same universality of spirit.

The Utopian families are careful that they have removed any element of discord among themselves before they come into a service of worship. They fear coming into temple with any unrelieved anxiety on their hearts.

Within the temple men sit on the right, women on the left. So as to insure that the children receive the most benefit from the service possible, the male children of each family take their place in temple in front of the mother. The Utopians think it important that the younger have always the oversight of adults.

Sacrifice of animals is never practiced in Utopian services. The logic behind this limitation is that the Divine Power has taken care to give life to creatures that they might enjoy it—it is not likely that the same Power would delight in the slaughter of that life.

Other facts that Hythloday gives about the services of worship among Utopians are these: 1) all who come to the temple are attired in white garments; 2) the priest conducting the service wears many-colored vestments, but his apparel is made from the feathers of birds rather than from gold or precious stones; 3) the congregation prostrate themselves as the priest appears in the vestibule of the temple; 4) when the priest instructs them, the congregation rises and sings praises to God (Hythloday says the music of the Utopians is unique in its deep expression of the natural feelings of the worshippers); 5) priest and people pray at the end of the service: the prayers are written so as to encourage active application in the lives of the people. In all of the Utopian prayers God is worshipped as sovereign Lord, His gifts are acknowledged, He is given thanksgiving for the commonwealth the Utopians enjoy and for the religion they are permitted to share, and the people ask that God's will may triumph in their lives and nation, whether His sovereign will means the continuance or the disruption of the commonwealth; the Utopians make their submission to God's will so complete that they do not ask even for the preservation of their own singleminded religious faith: they submit so completely to God's providential rule that they pray for a multiplicity of religious response if that is what He most desires. Finally, the Utopians pray that God may grant them an easy death, one that will come with swiftness at God's appointed time.

> **COMMENT:** In his work on heresies, More makes the following statement about the life of the Christian Church: it is probably the case that he was writing the passage with greater seriousness than that with which he was writing about the religion of the Utopians:
>
>> . . . if churches and congregations of Christian people resorting together to God's service were ones abolished and put away, we were like to have few good temples of God in many souls, but all would within a while wear

clean away and clearly fall to nought. And this prove we by experience, that those which be the best temples of God in their souls, they are most used to come to the temple of stone.

More's friend, Erasmus, took a somewhat different position and denounced princes who tried to shelter their crimes within stone edifices.

CONCLUSION: When Hythloday finishes his account of life in Utopia, he affirms that he considers that society the only one deserving of the name commonwealth.

> **COMMENT:**   One may correctly think of Hythloday's concept of a commonwealth as expressible in the words *common-good*. Humans must unite themselves in society because no one is complete in himself; every man needs other men. The *common-good* in such a commonwealth is that no one class is favored above any other—rather, all decisions of government have as their touchstone the greatest happiness for the greatest number. The evil of private property is precisely that the advantage of a single individual is set above the welfare of the whole community.

Hythloday explains in conclusion that because of the freedom of the Utopians from private want, they are able to involve themselves in serious consideration of the best state for human society. Explaining that Utopia has no citizen who is a rich man and no citizen who is a beggar, Hythloday states the paradox (and considering the way Hythloday has spoken of Utopia, one would feel he means it as a *divine* paradox) that "though no man has anything, yet every man is rich." A citizen is free to find joy and contentment in life, says Hythloday, if he knows that his wife and family are provided for and if he knows that the Utopian economy includes a built-in social security that insures freedom from want for the old and the disabled.

Hythloday asks his listeners to compare, therefore, the Utopian way of life with that of other nations, where, he says, he is at a loss to find equity and justice. He enumerates examples of the absence of such equity and justice in other societies: 1) persons whose work is unessential to the life of the commonwealth but enjoy luxury (goldsmiths, moneylenders); 2) persons who do the most essential work of the commonwealth live like beasts of burden (farmers, carpenters). Compared to the state of Utopia, life in other nations is a very sorry second best. The following is part of Hythloday's statement about any other commonwealth:

> But after it hath abused the labors of their [the people's] lusty and flowering age, at the last when they be oppressed with old age and sickness, being needy, poor, and indigent of all things, then forgetting their so many painful watchings, not remembering their so many and so great benefits, recompenseth and acquiteth them most unkindly with miserable death. And yet besides this the rich men not only by private fraud, but also by common laws, do every day pluck and snatch away from the poor some part of their daily living. So whereas it seemed before unjust to recompense with unkindness their pains that have been beneficial to the public weal [commonwealth], now they have to this their wrong and unjust dealing (which is yet a much worse point) given the name of justice, yea and that by the force of a law.

Hythloday in considering the commonwealths of the world with which he had been in his life associated says that he finds them in comparison to Utopia a kind of conspiracy among rich men. The men grow rich through the exploitation of the poor, and then with their economic power institute and enforce laws that make further exploitation legal under the guise of public benefit.

Hythloday contends that the most lamentable irony of it all is that even when they have locked up in their own storehouses possessions that would have been sufficient for the whole people, still the rich do not have the happiness in life that the Utopians enjoy. The destructive force in the life of a commonwealth is insistence on holding private property:

> . . . in that all the desire of money with the use thereof is utterly secluded and banished, how great a heap of cares is cut away! How great an occasion of wickedness and mis-

chief is plucked up by the roots! For who knoweth not, that fraud, theft, rapine, brawling, quarelling, disorders, strife, chiding, contention, murder, treason, poisoning, which by daily punishments are rather revenged than refrained do die when money dieth? And also that fear, grief, care, labors and watchings do perish even the very same moment that money perisheth?

The man who holds property in ownership becomes an enemy of the people. Money, the means of the *individual's* getting what *he* needs, becomes the means that prevents *all* men from having what *they* need. Hythloday illustrates this principle with the metaphor of the famine, which reduced the nation to want and misery because the granaries of *only a few men* were full. Hythloday thinks that if their vision could be cleared, even the rich men would prefer being sure of having the basics of life always provided than having an excess of goods to be responsible for: "how much better it were to lack no necessary thing, than to abound with overmuch superfluity."

The root of man's selfish hoarding, says Hythloday, is "that one only beast, the princess and mother of all mischief, pride. . . ." It is this demon that has been the sole cause for man's not having heretofore established in every commonwealth the very laws that make Utopia a place of human fulfillment. Some of the most astringent statements in *Utopia* are made by Hythloday when he speaks about the evil of pride:

> She [pride] measureth not wealth and prosperity by her own commodities, but by the misery and incommodities of other; she would not by her good will be made a goddess, if there were no wretches left, over whom she might, like a scornful lady, rule and triumph, over whose miseries her felicites might shine, whose poverty she might vex, torment and increase by gorgeously setting forth her riches. This hellhound creapeth into men's hearts, and plucketh them back from entering the right path of life, and is so deeply rooted in men's breasts, that she can not be plucked out.

The Utopians have found the best state for man because they

have been able to deal with the sin of pride, to dig ambition
and factionalism out of the human heart.

When Hythloday's discourse about Utopia ends, More assumes
the stance of finding some of his revelations about Utopia ab-
surd. The element of the Utopian scheme that More most ob-
jects to is the abolition of private property, "the community of
their life and living, without any occupying [exchange] of
money. . . ." This kind of economy, says More, would serve
to undermine all those features of a commonwealth that are
considered "true ornaments and honors"—"nobility, magnifi-
cence, worship, honor and majesty."

For whatever objections he has, however, More does end *Utopia*
with the confession that there are in the Utopian commonwealth
many features that he would wish to see in his own and in other
countries.

CRITICAL COMMENTARY

The dust of neglect has never settled on Thomas More's *Utopia,* not at any time during the four-hundred years the book has existed, and the dust has not been kept away by only dutiful scholarly reading. Delighted curiosity has been the response of More's readers, readers who have come to *Utopia* with the diversity of values and ideals of many different cultures. The very word *Utopian* has a currency in our language—although our use of the word is in a sense unfair to the intent of More's work—for both the dream of perfection and the realization of the futility of the dream.

As discussed in the introductory section, "The Genre of *Utopia,*" some readers have considered *Utopia* to be a carefully considered program, seriously intended as a programmatic work for the reconstruction of human society in England and elsewhere. Others have found *Utopia* to be a joke with barbs, designed in the typical Renaissance way to entertain but at the same time to instruct. Most of the more finely honed interpretations of *Utopia* come somewhere within these two large areas, whether *Utopia* is considered 1) a prophecy of an ideal social state that would come to pass in some glorious future, or 2) an actual blueprint for rebuilding England and Europe, or 3) a book of classical style, in the manner of Plato's *Republic,* or 4) a Christian humanist's dream of the best of all possible worlds with kings who are philosophers and a church that has been renewed from within, or 5) an effort to revive something of the original joy, triumph, and love of the pristine New Testament community, or 6) a mere escape through the imagination from the unpleasant realities of present time, or 7) a piece of social satire clothed in a fantastic story, or 8) merely a humanist's *jeu d'esprit* for the delight of fellow humanists.

The mass of critical work on *Utopia* has weighed the scales
down on the side of the religious ideas and attitudes in Utopia
and the communistic philosophy that pervades the Utopian
society. A few critics have asked questions about the importance of More's humanism to his composition of *Utopia*.
William Nelson of Columbia University has made some well-
founded observations on More's work as a humanist in relationship to his association with the Mercers' Company (see William
Nelson, "Thomas More, Grammarian and Orator," *PMLA,*
1943). J. H. Hexter in his perceptive book *More's Utopia, The
Biography of an Idea* (Princeton University Press, 1952) sharp-
ens the meaning of the name *humanist* for More by advancing
the clarifying name *Christian humanist*. With Erasmus and
other Christian humanists, More, says Hexter, shared the belief that in *both* the literature of the New Testament and early
Church fathers *and* in the literature of pagan antiquity, there
was a wisdom that could produce an improvement in men individually and in men corporately as they shared together mem-
bership in the Body of Christ in the world, the Christian Church.

But Hexter does not stop with More's humanism. He proceeds
to discuss *Utopia* as a book that seriously frames for man "the
Best Society." The basis of this Best Society is not the religion and philosophy of the Utopian society, Hexter clarifies,
although the religion and philosophy of Utopia are worthy of
the society; the real basis of the Best Society of *Utopia* is the
economic philosophy, specifically the abolition of private property, of a money economy. Frederic Seebohm is another of
More's critics who has concentrated on his interest in humanistic reform (see Frederic Seebohm, *The Oxford Reformers,*
Everyman's Library, 1914).

Russell Ames in his *Citizen Thomas More and His Utopia*
(Princeton University Press, 1949) has analyzed More as a reformer within the political and economic conditions of his time.
Ames takes More's Utopian communism seriously and thinks
that More's book is gravely concerned with the social evils that
come from prevailing economic practices and conditions in
More's time. Ames regrets the lack of stress that has been given
to the communism of the early Christian Church and to the
"more or less radical economic character of northern humanism," both weighty influences on More's thought and work.

Among the works that have been concerned seriously with More's economics is Karl Kautsky's *Thomas More and His Utopia* (translated by H. J. Stenning, New York, 1927). Kautsky studied More within the English middle class of the times, especially with respect to More's relationship to London merchants. Kautsky found that More was a socialist of modern type, that the ideal of *Utopia* anticipated modern socialism. Russell Ames has criticized Kautsky for projecting his own controlling concerns into the past, and for incorrectly assuming that capitalism had come to dominate English society in More's time.

Perhaps the most famous of the relatively recent books on More is R. W. Chambers' *Thomas More* (The University of Michigan Press, First edition as an Ann Arbor Paperback in 1958). Chambers does not discuss Kautsky's work on More. But Russell Ames remarks that Chambers' discussion of *Utopia* refutes at least by implication Kautsky's position. Chambers' book is more oriented to personal elements in More's life and work, and tends at times through eloquence and charm to subdue the reader's power to make an objective appraisal of More. Chambers interprets Thomas More as a reformer, but a reformer of medieval values and principles. Chambers calls attention to the important difference between the reformer of the Protestant persuasion (we may think of Martin Luther as an example) who wished to place the Holy Scriptures in every man's hands, so that each man might be able to read the Bible for himself, and the reform measures of King Utopus who administered reform in the Island of Utopia according to medieval laws. Chambers refers for one element of support for his argument to William Morris, "our great Utopian of the Nineteenth Century," who said that Thomas More belonged to the medieval world to a much greater degree than he belonged to the world of the Renaissance.

One of the most erudite and eloquent literary critics of our times, Professor C. S. Lewis, in a book that surveys the sixteenth century (its non-dramatic literature only) with great scope and depth (*English Literature in the Sixteenth Century Excluding Drama,* Oxford at the Clarendon Press, 1959) analyzes *Utopia* as a dialogue in which it is not possible to settle which of the opinions expressed, if any, is More's own. Lewis holds, and with sturdy support from the literature of More's time, that *Utopia* can only be a confused book if More intended it as a philosophical treatise with a consistently serious intent and argument. Lewis says that *Utopia* will make sense only when we read it as a prod, a goad that jumps many rabbits out of hiding but shoots none.

ESSAY QUESTIONS AND ANSWERS

1. What is the main theme of Utopia?

ANSWER: The inscriptions written for each of the two books in *Utopia* will show that the overall theme of the work is the best state for a commonwealth, the best structure for a society in which man may live with his fellow men and find fulfillment. At the very heart of the content of *Utopia* is Hythloday's repeated message that the best form of government for a nation of men, for a commonwealth, cannot exist so long as individuals are obsessed with the desire for private property. This desire must be replaced by the concern for the welfare of *all* men, and this concern can find its best, its most effective expression in a community where *all* things are enjoyed in common ownership. The paradox (in several places he seems to speak of it as a *divine* paradox) of Hythloday's message is that every citizen in Utopia has what he needs because no man owns anything. Hythloday's message about the abolition of private ownership in Utopia occupies two-thirds of the book. The debate on royal councilorship in Book I is integrally related to the question of what makes up the best state for man. The debate reveals the potential failures of princes who rule over men, and, in process, the probable failure of a man who gives his strength to the counseling of princes.

2. What were More's practical involvements at the time *Utopia* was written?

ANSWER: The foremost of the guilds of London was the Mercers' Company. More had had a connection with that corporation since 1508. When economic relations between England and Flanders became acutely strained in 1514, his association with the Mercers in addition to his other public responsibilities made him the logical choice for a diplomatic mission to the Low Countries. Since the thirteenth century English wool had been transported to Flanders for processing into cloth. English merchants now faced the disruption of this most important source of income. Thomas More was chosen for the corps of diplomats who went to the Low Countries in May of 1515 to heal this economic wound. Needless to say, it was a situation requiring the most deft diplomatic touch. More's mission to Flanders is of particular interest to the reader of *Utopia,* for it was there that More wrote the second book of the work. Book II was written first. The references that one finds at the beginning of Book I are from the experiences of the mission to Flanders. More tells us there that the first meeting with the Flemish deputies took place in Bruges; from there they went to Brussels; having found it impossible to reach agreement on the matters at hand, they next traveled to Antwerp, where More met the exceedingly excellent Peter Giles, the town clerk of Antwerp. As he remained abroad for the largest part of 1515, the author of *Utopia* was pressed with the question of whether or not to give himself to full-time service to the court of Henry VIII. The man who had already written passionately against the indulgent privileges granted autocratic princes would have had to have prolonged strife with the morals of the matter. The King and Cardinal Wolsey, chief minister and papal legate in England, had made efforts to persuade More to enter the royal court and its politics. Despite his frequent service to the Government, his numerous embassies, and his frequent honors, More was reluctant to be drawn into the vortex of ambition and vanity that any royal court must necessarily be. But anyone who had read More's earlier work, even the early epigrams he wrote while studying Latin, would know that his consciousness of the graft-ridden exploitation of the weak by the strong would overpower any inclination he felt to preserve private spiritual excellence in a life of restraint. More had by 1516 already seen too much of the evil results of rule by selfish men. It was during these months of decision about royal service that More was thinking of Book I, which was written in the spring or summer of 1516.

3. What is the historical setting that More gives for the events related in *Utopia*; that is, where does he say he met Peter Giles, and how did he get to know Raphael Hythloday?

ANSWER: At the beginning of Book I More explains his commission to Flanders at the command of Henry VIII. The reason for the embassy was to discuss various aspects of the strained commercial relations of English and Flemish merchants regarding the export of English wool to Flanders for processing into cloth. When business led More to Antwerp, he had the great pleasure of meeting Peter Giles, who became to More a most perfect friend. More pays the highest compliments to him for his erudition, for his character, for his loyalty, for his sincerity. In the early paragraphs of *Utopia* More explains that Giles was responsible for relieving his loneliness for home and family. By way of an introduction provided by Peter Giles, More meets Raphael Hythloday. The meeting occurs as More is returning to his lodgings from attending mass at Notre Dame. Giles tells More of Hythloday's travels with Amerigo Vespucci, to "know the far countries of the world." After More and Hythloday had introduced themselves one to another, they sat down in the garden of the house where More was staying, so More informs us, and began to talk together. More says that it is not the concern of his book to relate what Hythloday said of each of his adventures, but that his purpose in *Utopia* is to give account of what Hythloday said "of the manners, customs, laws, and ordinances of the Utopians."

4. To what genre (type) of literature does *Utopia* belong?

ANSWER: A genre of literature popular in More's time was the mock oration, a kind of rhetorical exercise. In the rhetorical schools of the time the most standard literary practice was to write in praise of something in a mock way. One of the most famous of the works of this type was written by More's friend Erasmus and was titled *The Praise of Folly*. Erasmus' work was no doubt one of the stimuli that caused More to write *Utopia. The Praise of Folly* is a kind of learned jest, but it is not all jest: toward the end of the book Folly's oration finishes on a very serious note—the oration concludes with an indictment of worldly wisdom in the paradoxical terms that folly is wisdom, and wisdom is folly. More's *Utopia* belongs to the same genre. It is also a learned jest. *Utopia* is not either a program-matic book nor a prophetic book. *Utopia* belongs to that wealth of sixteenth-century literature that we may call mirror literature, literature written so that the reader may be better able to see himself in bold relief against other persons, other persons act-ing in situations that he may or may not actually confront him-self. More is not advocating a body of principles and laws that England should adopt, but he is thinking that his countrymen might be able in reading *Utopia* to see their weakness more sharply delineated. More in writing *Utopia* was not hoping for any wholesale reform of Christian Europe—he was not laying down definite guidelines for a religious and political reformation on a large scale—but he did hope that some men would come to beneficial changes as a result of comparing themselves to Utopians.

5. How do some of the names of persons and places and some of the characteristics of life in Utopia reveal More's literary technique?

ANSWER: The very name of the Island (and the work, of course) is a combination of Greek elements meaning "nowhere." The name *Utopus* (name of the founder of the government of the Island) is derived from the Greek *ou*, meaning "not," and the Greek *topos*, meaning "place, position, spot." King Utopus was ruler over noplace. If one considers the geography of the world of Utopia, one will realize that a line drawn from Utopia through the center of the earth to the other side would come out at the place of the globe where England is located. The name Hythloday means "expert in trifles," or "well-learned in non-sense." The name is made up of the Greek word *huthlos*, mean-ing "idle talk," or "nonsense," and the Greek word *daios*, meaning "knowing," or "cunning." It is possible that More chose Raphael because the name had been interpreted as mean-ing "the healing of God": Raphael Hythloday might be thought of as an instrument of salvation for Christian Europe through the fantastic things that he tells Peter Giles and Thomas More. The name of the river in Utopia, Anyder, is formed from Greek words meaning "waterless." One may think of the shape of the Island of Utopia: it is circular, and the circle in geometric lore has always been considered the most perfect figure; England, on the contrary, is shaped like a triangle, and the triangle in geometric lore is the most imperfect figure. Many such parallels of contrast may be found in *Utopia*. The most precious metal in England, gold, is used in Utopia for chamber pots; the bridge near the Capital City of Utopia does not interfere with river traffic as does the London Bridge; in Utopia there are few priests, and they are holy, whereas in England there are many who are not holy. It is obvious that More in writing *Utopia* is playing—but the essential question is: *What kind of game?* The best way to read *Utopia* is to think of the book as an upside-down game with an ultimately serious purpose. In the Utopian world of opposites, we have a series of mirrors held opposite to us, so that we may be better able to know ourselves for what we truly are.

ADDITIONAL QUESTIONS FOR REVIEW:

6. What does More mean by the word *commonwealth?*

7. On what grounds does More in Book I advise Hythloday to enter royal councilorship?

8. What dramatic settings does Hythloday use for refuting More's argument, and what does each setting demonstrate?

9. Give ten features of the geography and topography of the Island of Utopia.

10. Explain the function and methods of agriculture in Utopia.

11. Describe the governmental structure in Utopia.

12. What is the Utopian idea about property?

13. What are some of the most grievous consequences of enclosures that Hythloday names?

14. What are the conditions that the Utopians consider necessary for a life of genuine fulfillment?

15. For what reasons will the Utopians go to war?

16. What is the Utopian view of euthanasia?

17. What is the Utopian practice with regard to slavery?

18. Name some of the methods of warfare used by the Utopians.

19. What several religious beliefs did King Utopus require of his people when he took over the government of the Island?

20. Explain the Utopian worship services, and name what they consider the principal results of religious faith in life.

BIBLIOGRAPHY AND GUIDE TO FURTHER RESEARCH

EDITIONS OF *UTOPIA*

Collins, J. Churton. *Sir Thomas More's Utopia*. Oxford: The Clarendon Press, 1930. Reprints Ralph Robynson's translation of 1551, with Robynson's spelling. Full and useful notes, probably second only to the Yale edition of *Utopia* by Surtz and Hexter, mentioned below. Collins' introduction to *Utopia* is still helpful, though again not nearly as comprehensive as the Yale edition.

Gallagher, Ligeia. *More's Utopia and Its Critics*. Fair Lawn, New Jersey: Scott, Foresman and Company, 1964. A casebook for student use. The book, in paperback for an economical price, is designed especially for student research. Here is no doubt the best copy of the *Utopia* for the student to buy, this side of the Yale edition by Surtz and Hexter. This is a reliable translation of *Utopia* with modernized spelling. Besides giving the comment of five sixteenth-century figures on More and his work, the editor has selected some of the best of recent criticism on *Utopia*. Suggestions for research papers.

Lupton, J. H. *The Utopia of Sir Thomas More*. Oxford: The Clarendon Press, 1895. Robynson's translation of *Utopia* with notes by Lupton, but the notes are not as extensive as those of Collins (or, of course, Surtz and Hexter). But Lupton's introduction (again much briefer than Surtz and Hexter) is sound and instructive on historical conditions surrounding the writing of *Utopia*.

Milligan, Burton A. *Three Renaissance Classics*. New York:

Charles Scribner's Sons, 1953. Machiavelli's *The Prince,* More's *Utopia,* and Castiglione's *The Courtier* in one volume. A useful edition for the student who would like to pursue some of More's concerns in two other famous Renaissance works and carry it all under one binding.

Surtz, Edward and J. H. Hexter. *The Complete Works of St. Thomas More, Volume 4.* New Haven: Yale University Press, 1965. This is the fourth and the most recent volume of the *Yale Complete Works,* to be presented in fourteen volumes. The student will find very nearly everything he needs in this one volume. The introduction brings together in well-defined divisions the results of the best scholarship on *Utopia* to date. What the introduction does not provide, the notes do: 303 pages of notes comment on, explain, and document just about everything More said in *Utopia,* and the layout of the book is such that everything can be found easily. More's Latin text on one side, and the translation, a new, modern one, on the facing page.

Warrington, John. *More's Utopia and A Dialogue of Comfort.* New York: E. P. Dutton & Co., Inc., 1962. This is a volume of the Everyman's Library. Warrington writes a brief, pithy introduction and then updates the spelling of Robynson's translation.

BIOGRAPHY OF THOMAS MORE

Bolt, Robert. *A Man for All Seasons.* New York: Random House, 1962. Bolt is not interested in writing this play about More as Christian, or as Christian saint, within the historical circumstances of the period—except insofar as this approach is involved in his primary reason for writing about More: namely, Thomas More as a man, a man with an astounding knowledge of himself and of his reasons for being alive.

Bridgett, T. E. *The Life of Blessed Thomas More.* London: Burns, Oates & Washbourne, Ltd., 1924. One of the merits of this good biography is the profuse quotation from More's writings. There are helpful, interesting appendices on More's family background and his descendants.

Chambers, R. W. *Thomas More*. Ann Arbor, Michigan: The University of Michigan Press, 1958. The standard modern biography. Chambers is a non-Catholic scholar, and his book is famous for its lack of bias. Careful indexing makes this biography especially useful for students who are writing papers. Chambers is often eloquent. The book has been criticized for a lack of attention to More as a practical man with a career.

Froude, J. A. *Life and Letters of Erasmus*. London: Longmans, Green and Company, 1895. There is no doubting the importance of the friendship between Erasmus and More for the lives and work of both men. Erasmus' great friend comes more clearly before our eyes through Mr. Froude's presentation of the interaction of the two about whom the author says, "no two men ever suited each other better. . . ."

Roper, William. *The Life of Sir Thomas More*, ed. E. V. Hitchcock. London: Oxford University Press, 1935. Written by More's son-in-law, the character of this biography is more dramatic than historical. Roper writes out of too much devotion for More and too long after the events he describes to be trusted on details. But from reading Roper's *Life* we can have a richer comprehension of the whole man.

Routh, E. M. G. *Sir Thomas More and His Friends, 1477-1535*. New York: Russell & Russell, Inc., 1963. One of the most readable studies of More. The book, as the title might suggest, is especially sensitive to history. One of its strengths is the intelligent, discriminating collection of quotations from More's writings and other documents closely related to his labors and longings.

CRITICAL WORKS ON THOMAS MORE, *UTOPIA* AND THE TIMES

Adams, Robert Pardee. *The Better Part of Valor: More, Erasmus, Colet, and Vives on Humanism, War, and Peace, 1496-1535*. Seattle: University of Washington Press, 1962. Of course clarifying on what it means to call More a *humanist,* the book is informational in the reactions it presents from other humanists to the important historical

events in the early sixteenth century. In the notes and
bibliography there is an expansive collection of suggestions
for further study and research. One should exercise cau-
tion with regard to Mr. Adams' position that More be-
lieved England could become a utopia if there were a wise
prince to lead the government.

Allen, J. W. *A History of Political Thought in the Sixteenth
Century*. New York: Barnes and Noble, Inc., 1960. Pub-
lished as a "University Paperback." The book contains an
examination of More's reaction to the Protestant revolution against the Catholic Church. More permitted himself
to be killed as a protest against forces that threatened to
destroy true religion.

Allen, P. S. *The Age of Erasmus*. Oxford: Oxford University
Press, 1914. Clarifies More's relationship to the printing
of *Utopia*. The reader should beware Mr. Allen's remarks
on matters relating to More's marriage and his conduct
before marriage.

Ames, Russell. *Citizen Thomas More and His Utopia*. Princeton: Princeton University Press, 1949. An examination of
Thomas More within his practical involvements, this book
proves to be corrective to the position taken by R. W.
Chambers. Ames brings his knowledge of More as a man
involved in business and politics to bear on *Utopia* and
decides that the work is a product of an attack made by a
capitalistic economy on feudalism.

Bouyer, Louis. *Erasmus and His Times*. Maryland: The New-
man Press, 1959. More is a man of the Renaissance, a
great figure because he was a man not only of contemplation but also of action. Thoughtful presentation of More's
humor.

Campbell, W. E. *More's Utopia and His Social Teaching*. London: Eyre and Spottiswoode, Ltd., 1930. One reviewer has
called attention to the *and* in the title of this book: whereas
Utopia, Campbell thinks, is seriously concerned with reform, we do not find in the work the total of More's ideas
about what a commonwealth should be. *Utopia* should be
read in conjunction with later works by More.

Caspari, Fritz. *Humanism and the Social Order in Tudor England.* Chicago: University of Chicago Press, 1954. This book is probably not dependable in calling *Utopia* a "programmatic work" such as Thomas Elyot's *The Book Named the Governor.* But the book tells much on the all-important subject of humanism and on More as one of its founders in England.

Donner, H. W. *Introduction to Utopia.* London: Sidgwick and Jackson, Ltd., 1945. Donner suggests sources for *Utopia,* stresses the importance of *Utopia* as a work written in Latin, attacks the idea that *Utopia* is advocatory of revolution, recommends a reading of *Utopia* as a grand collection of imaginative insights rather than as a program of practical directives.

Hexter, J. H. *More's Utopia: The Biography of an Idea.* Princeton: Princeton University Press, 1952. Hexter has been much complimented for his independent interpretations based on thorough scholarship. This book includes a study of the construction of *Utopia* as a literary work, an examination of the dates of its composition, and a survey of opinion by a number of the critics of *Utopia.* Hexter considers *Utopia* to be seriously intended by More as a criticism of his society.

Huizinga, J. *Erasmus and the Age of Reformation.* New York: Harper & Brothers, 1957. The issues at stake between the Biblically-oriented Protestant Reformers and the Church-oriented Catholic Reformers are presented. Both Erasmus and More were suspicious of men who were turning away from centuries of worship and work. One wonders if More would have been so generous with the freedom of faith and life granted the Utopians if he had known what was to happen because of Martin Luther.

Kautsky, Karl. *Thomas More and His Utopia,* trans. H. J. Stenning. London: A. & C. Black, Ltd., 1927. This book is most instructive in its revelations about More's relation to the economics of his time: More was a trenchant analyst and philosopher of economic theory. But, Kautsky is guilty of exaggerated strictures against More's theological beliefs and his subsequent position in Church tradition.

Kautsky probably also reads More too much from the vantage point of modern socialism.

Surtz, Edward. *The Praise of Pleasure; Philosophy, Education, and Communism in More's Utopia.* Cambridge, Mass.: Harvard University Press, 1957. This book and the one listed below are by one of the editors of the new Yale edition of *Utopia.*

————. *The Praise of Wisdom; A Commentary on the Religious and Moral Problems and Background of St. Thomas More's Utopia.* Chicago: Loyola University Press, 1957.

BIBLIOGRAPHICAL WORKS

Gibson, R. W. *St. Thomas More: A Preliminary Bibliography of His Works and of Moreana to the Year 1750.* New Haven: Yale University Press, 1961.

Sullivan, Frank and M. P. *Moreana, 1478-1945.* Kansas City: Rockhurst College, 1946. The editors call this "A Preliminary Check List of Material by and about Saint Thomas More." The word *Preliminary* was used for the reason that a more comprehensive bibliography by the same editors was issued in 1964 and 1965. (See below.)

Sullivan, Frank and Majie Padberg. *Moreana, Material for the Study of Saint Thomas More.* Los Angeles: Loyola University of Los Angeles, 1964 & 1965. As the dates cited indicate, there are two volumes of this work, the first covering authors and editors with names beginning *A-F,* the second *G-M.* This work is one of the most helpful tools that the student could use in doing research on More. Both volumes are not only bibliography in the sense of a collection of books, but they are profusely annotated bibliographies. Further, not only do they offer in very nearly every case a full summary of the work cited, but they offer also reviews of the criticism written about the work cited. For persons interested in Thomas More, these two volumes would be a good buy: reading them through would give the student a substantial education in More and his works. Future volumes are planned for remaining authors and reviewers.

NOTES

MONARCH® *NOTES AND STUDY GUIDES*

ARE AVAILABLE AT RETAIL STORES EVERYWHERE

In the event your local bookseller cannot provide you with other Monarch titles you want—

ORDER ON THE FORM BELOW:

Complete order form appears on inside front & back covers for your convenience.

Simply send retail price, local sales tax, if any, plus 25¢ to cover mailing & handling.

IBM #	AUTHOR & TITLE	(exactly as shown on title listing)	PRICE
	PLUS ADD'L FOR POSTAGE		25¢
	GRAND TOTAL		

MONARCH® **PRESS,** a division of Simon & Schuster, Inc.
Mail Service Department, 1 West 39th Street, New York, N.Y. 10018

I enclose................................dollars to cover retail price, local sales tax, plus mailing and handling.

Name_____

(Please print)

Address_____

City_____State_____Zip_____

Please send check or money order. We cannot be responsible for cash.